PETER, THE REVOLUTIONARY TSAR

PETER,
The Revolutionary Tsar

by **PETER BROCK PUTNAM**

Maps and Illustrations by Laszlo Kubinyi

HARPER & ROW, PUBLISHERS

New York   Evanston   San Francisco   London

To my fabulous wife, Durinda, who provided the intellectual companionship and emotional climate that made this book possible.

TABLE OF CONTENTS

Table of Contents

ACKNOWLEDGMENTS

I wish to acknowledge my gratitude to the staffs of the Firestone Library at Princeton, the Widener Library at Harvard, the Boston Public Library, and the Slavonic Division of the New York Public Library for their helpfulness.

I owe much to the kindness of Mary Dunn in lending me invaluable books from her private library, and to the extraordinary generosity of G. Peter Fleck in arranging a visit to the cottage Peter the Great occupied during his brief sojourn in Zaandam.

I am deeply indebted to Jerome Blum, Joseph R. Strayer, and Ashley Montagu for their reading and criticism of the manuscript.

No words can express my indebtedness to my wife, but I would like to pay special tribute to the dedication and reading skills of the volunteers of Recording for the Blind, Inc., whose articulate reading of several scholarly volumes were extremely important to the writing of this book. Their tape recordings of educational materials make the tools of research and scholarship available to many blind students, professionals, and writers like myself.

A NOTE ON NAMES, PLACES, AND DATES

This book is addressed, not to scholars, but to the general public. For this reason, the system for adapting names from the Russian alphabet is the one recommended for use with the general public in J. Thomas Shaw's *The Transliteration of Modern Russian for English-Language Publications* (Madison: University of Wisconsin Press, 1967). However, there are several exceptions. With place names like Moscow or Archangel, long familiar to the American public in their anglicized form, I have retained that form in preference to Moscva or Archangelsk. For the same reason, I have preferred Peter to Petr and Alexis to Alexei. Finally, I have omitted the feminine endings on the surnames of women, because their inclusion might cause confusion.

Many place names have been changed since Peter's day. Nizhni-Novgorod is now Gorky. Tsaritsyn became Stalingrad and later Volgograd. Occasionally, the modern names are appended in parentheses, but, in general, this practice seemed more distracting than enlightening. The old German name for the river that runs through Riga is Düna, and I have retained it in preference to the Slavic Dvina, too easily confused with the Northern Dvina which empties into the White Sea at Archangel.

Peter adopted a western calendar, but he chose the Julian rather than the Gregorian calendar in use today. The Julian calendar, often designated "old style," had lost ten days to the Gregorian, or "new style," calendar by the seventeenth century, and this became eleven days after 1700. The dates in this book have been corrected to the Gregorian (or modern) calendar. Thus, Peter's birthday is dated June 9, new style, rather than May 30, old style. To reckon the dates old style, it is only necessary to subtract ten days from any date appearing in the seventeenth century, or eleven days for those in the eighteenth century.

Peter Brock Putnam, 1972

BOOK ONE

The Path to Power

Chapter 1

A PEOPLE DIVIDED

At five o'clock on the morning of June 9, 1672, the enormous bell known to the people of Moscow as Great Ivan began to toll. The northern sun was already well above the horizon, glinting on the gilt crosses and onion domes that rose above the blood-red brick battlements of the Kremlin. Its fortress walls enclosed a triangle, a half mile on a side, but the clang of Great Ivan's metal throat seemed to shout in the ear of everyone within.

They heard it in the outer city, too—in the great market-place of the Kitaygorod, where boys with trays of hot meat pies cried their wares before the shopmen's stalls, and across the river in the Streltsy Quarter, where bearded soldiers in flowing red, green, or purple caftans were on their way to mass. The pealing of the bell carried into the Bielgorod or White Town, where roosters crowed and pigs squealed in their fenced yards. It penetrated the log walls of peasant huts and the brick and stone façades of noble palaces. As far as the earth and timber ramparts that surrounded the city, and even beyond, the brazen voice of Great Ivan proclaimed the news that Tsaritsa Natalia had borne the Tsar Alexis their first child, a Tsarevich who would be called Peter.

Since one o'clock in the morning, there had been comings and goings in the Kremlin. Messengers were dispatched to all the leading personages in the city and surrounding countryside. The Tsar had decreed a solemn procession and service of thanksgiving for the birth of his son, and he summoned his loyal subjects to attend.

By midday, a great multitude had assembled in the Red Square before the palace of the Tsar. At the head of the procession marched the chief dignitaries of the church— the Metropolitan with the archbishops, bishops, and abbots. They wore jewel-encrusted crowns and cloth of gold, and they carried sacred ikons and fluttering banners. Next came the great magnates and ministers, followed by the colonels of the army. Here marched the Tsar himself, accompanied by the princes of the royal family. The princesses, too, were there, invisible behind canopies that screened them from the public view. Bringing up the rear were deputations of the merchants and of the craft guilds.

The sunlight flashed on flowing robes of bright silk and brocade, rich furs, pearl-studded caps, and boots of embroidered felt and fine leather. The splendor and solemnity of the spectacle amid the domed palaces and cathedrals gave the impression that the realm of Muscovy was wholeheartedly united behind its sovereign. But in truth, its people were deeply divided.

On an island in the White Sea, six hundred miles to the north, the monks of the Solovetsky Monastery were openly defying the troops of the Tsar. In the provinces, whole villages lay in ashes, put to the torch as a protest against the religious innovations decreed in Moscow. On the southern steppes, Cossack frontiersmen sang folk ballads in praise of the heroic Stenka Razin, the leader of the greatest peasant rebellion in Russian history until his death the year before.

The hatred that divided the people at the birth of the Tsarevich Peter had its roots deep in the Muscovite past. To understand it, we must go back to a time before the land was known as Muscovy, when Kiev and not Moscow was the capital of Russia.

In the ninth century, Viking bands of warrior traders sailed down the Dnieper River and subjugated the primitive Slavs who had migrated from central Europe much earlier. Followers of the legendary Rurik, they were known as Rus, and the region acquired the name of Russia. They built the fortified towns of Kiev, Smolensk, and Novgorod and struck up a trade with Constantinople down the river and across the Black Sea.

As capital of the Byzantine Empire, Constantinople was a second Rome, and commerce with it led to cultural contacts. Christian missionaries came to Russia. One of them adapted the Greek alphabet to the Slavonic tongue to give Russia its first written language. In 988, Vladimir, the Grand Prince of Kiev, was converted to Greek Orthodoxy, the eastern form of Christianity.

The conversion made Kiev Russia an eastern frontier of Europe. Constantinople was the dominant religious and cultural influence. But there was contact with western

Europe as well. Kiev traded over the Baltic as well as the Black Sea, and its ruling families intermarried with western royalty.

Then, in 1240, contact with Europe was suddenly severed. The Golden Horde of the Mongol Empire swept across Russia into central Europe. Commerce with Constantinople ceased. The Teutonic Knights took advantage of Russian helplessness to conquer her Baltic coast, and contact with the west was also severed. Russia was transformed from a frontier to an island of European culture. She was isolated from the west for four and a half centuries. She was excluded from the Renaissance and the Reformation, and most of the extraordinary cultural, economic, and social changes that accompanied them.

The collective experience of the Russian people during this period was like that of a child abandoned to shift for itself in the wilderness. While her European brothers and sisters were learning new arts and sciences, crafts and professions, Russia grew up as an untaught outcast in the northern forest. Yet she did grow up, and from her own problems and experiences, she developed an identity and a culture uniquely her own.

The new capital was Moscow. In the great days of Kiev, it had been only a tiny frontier settlement, but after the Mongol Conquest, the Russian people began a gradual migration to the north and east. They penetrated virgin forests and floated along great rivers. They fished, hunted, and trapped for furs. They felled trees, built log cabins, and planted in the clearings. Their advance was accompanied by the founding of scores of new monasteries, raised like religious fortresses, on the northern and eastern frontiers, from the Troitsa Monastery near Moscow to the

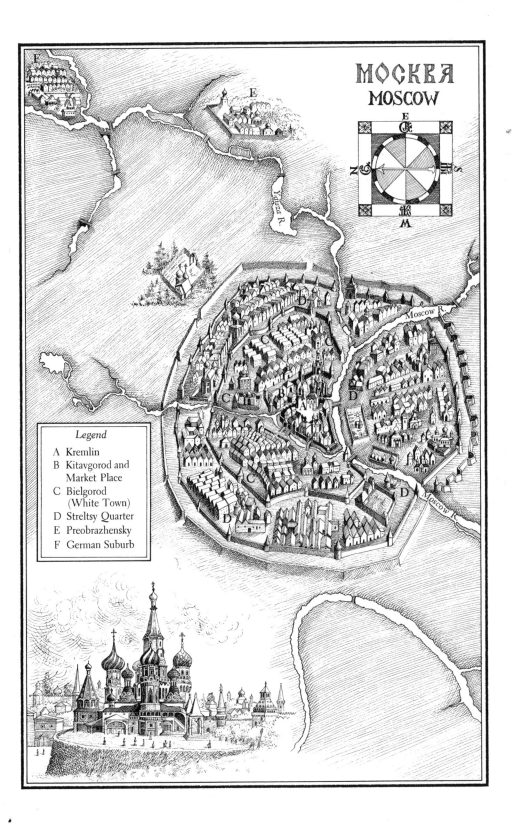

МОСКВА
MOSCOW

Legend
A Kremlin
B Kitavgorod and
  Market Place
C Bielgorod
  (White Town)
D Streltsy Quarter
E Preobrazhensky
F German Suburb

Solovetsky Monastery on the White Sea. By the end of
the fourteenth century, this migration had brought Moscow from the edge to the center of Russian population.
After 1326, when it became the residence of the Metropolitan, then the highest dignitary of the Russian Church,
it was also the religious center of the country.

The rise of Moscow was greatly aided by its remarkable
ruling family. The Mongol conquerors did not trouble
themselves to govern Russia. Their principal concern was
for tribute, and they appointed native underlings to de-
liver it to them in their distant capital of Sarai on the lower
Volga. It was as tax gatherers for the Golden Horde that
the rulers of Moscow began their rise. They were appointed
Grand Princes as a reward for their services. Shrewd, energetic, and ruthless, they used their privileged position with
the Mongols to subjugate the surrounding nobles. Then
they turned against their pagan overlords.

The Russian people were passionately Orthodox, and
their struggle for independence under the Grand Princes
of Moscow assumed the character of a crusade against the
infidel. It continued for more than a century with many
vicissitudes. In 1453, the fall of Constantinople to heathen
Turks threatened the total extinction of Greek Orthodox
Christendom. The second Rome, the capital of the Byzantine Empire, the light of the world, had fallen to the
powers of darkness.

But in 1480, this momentary eclipse served only to high-
light the glorious victory of Ivan the Great in expelling
the Golden Horde. The One True Faith had a new cham-
pion. Through his marriage to the niece of the last Byzan-

tine Emperor, Ivan now claimed to be his successor. He took the double-headed eagle of the Empire as his seal and assumed the title of Tsar, a Russianized form of Caesar. He was hailed as the only truly Christian monarch of the only truly Christian people. Moscow, his capital, was proclaimed as the third and final Rome. Like the first Rome, it gave its name to the state. Russia became known as Muscovy.

Muscovy's overriding problem was military. She was surrounded by formidable and warlike neighbors, and her geography offered no natural barriers against attack. She was invaded repeatedly by Mongols, Tartars, Turks, Poles, Lithuanians, Germans, and Swedes. Tartars burned Moscow in 1571. Poles occupied it in 1610.

Muscovy solved her formidable military problem by developing a centralized military autocracy that subjugated the peasants to the nobles and the nobles to the Tsar. Unlike earlier rulers in feudal Europe, the Tsar could not allow his great nobles or boyars to live as independent princes on their hereditary estates. To bring them to heel, Ivan the Great and his successors created new classes of lesser nobles called "men of service." These service nobles were allowed rights to estates granted by the Tsar only as long as they continued in his service. If they left his service or disobeyed the Tsar, their lands reverted to the crown, and for this reason they were far more responsive to the will of the Tsar than the boyars, who owned land outright.

Earlier Tsars reduced the power of the boyars. In 1565 Ivan the Terrible attacked them openly. Agreeing with an adviser that "A realm without terror is like a horse without a bridle," he created a special class of service nobles, the storm troopers of their day, and unleashed a reign of terror that lasted seven years. Literally thousands lost their lives, and the country was ravaged, but Ivan established beyond a doubt that the Tsar had the right to demand military service from all his nobles, great or small.

At the same time, the peasants were being forced into the service of noble landlords. During the period of the northeastern migration, a great deal of land had been pioneered and settled by free peasants, but in the sixteenth century, the Tsars granted these free lands to their service nobles, and the once-free peasants were obliged to perform farm labor for their lords. They were forbidden to leave their lord's land, and those who fled were hunted down by the troops of the Tsar. As the peasants sank into serfdom, their occasional savage uprisings were even more savagely suppressed. The advance of the Muscovite frontier meant the spread, not of freedom, but of serfdom.

The bolder serfs took refuge in flight beyond the frontier into the deserted steppes along the Dnieper, Don, and Ural Rivers. Here, many of them intermarried with Tartars and formed independent communities of Cossacks. "Cossack" is derived from a Turkish word meaning "free spirit" or "adventurer." The Cossacks remained true to the Russian religion, but they elected their own chiefs and fiercely resisted the attempts of the central government in Moscow to limit their freedom.

Serfs hated landlords, and Cossacks hated the central government, but all Russians hated non-Russians. Their xenophobia, or hatred of foreigners, was the reverse side of devotion to the One True Faith. Russians hated Turks and Tartars as non-Christians. They hated Catholics and

Protestants as false Christians. Unfortunately, Muscovy needed the technical skill of westerners to solve its military problems. Russians knew very little about modern fortification. Therefore, the walls of the Kremlin, the bastion of the third Rome, were designed by an Italian "heretic." Italian and Dutch gun founders cast Muscovite cannon, and Danish artillery experts played a key role in the conquest of Kazan.

In 1553, an English ship in search of a northeast passage to India landed in Archangel on the White Sea, establishing the first all-water route to Russia since the time of Kiev. Soon, English and Dutch ships were arriving every summer to exchange the products of western shops and factories for those of Russian farms and forests. They brought first a trickle, then a stream of visitors from northern Europe.

To the Russians, all the people of northern Europe were "Germans." They were called *nemtsy*, literally "dumb ones" or "dummies," because they spoke no Russian, but they made fine soldiers. Peter's father, Tsar Alexis, recruited thousands of "German" mercenaries for his war with Poland. To attract them, he had to offer special privileges and higher salaries than he paid his own subjects. They rose in the ranks of the service nobility. They were even permitted to build a Lutheran church in their special quarter outside Moscow. Devout Russians were incensed by such favors to heretics.

Greek Orthodoxy had been imported into Russia a thousand years after the birth of Jesus as a fully developed religious system, and the Russian people swallowed it whole. They were devout, superstitious, and extremely literal.

Their concern was for form, rather than content, for mystery rather than morality. They committed every last detail of the religious ritual to memory and performed it in all its changeless perfection and beauty for generations on end.

Then, in the reign of Tsar Alexis, something dreadful happened. After centuries of isolation, renewed contacts with the churchmen of Kiev and other old centers of Greek Orthodoxy revealed that certain impurities had crept into the Russian ritual. Horrified, Nikon, whom Alexis had appointed Patriarch or head of the Russian Church, determined to eliminate them.

To a modern observer, Nikon's "reforms" seem trivial, but they were earthshaking to Muscovy's ignorant and superstitious believers. A single change in the wording of the *Lord's Prayer* or in the spelling of Jesus seemed blasphemous to them. They were outraged by Nikon's command that the sign of the cross be made with three fingers instead of two. Three fingers were used for "making a fig," a coarse gesture of the streets, like thumbing your nose. To cross yourself with three fingers would be like thumbing your nose at the Lord God. Pious believers refused passionately.

Patriarch Nikon insisted just as passionately, and he had enlisted the autocratic power of the Tsar. Pious Russians were deeply attached to their religious paintings or ikons. Even the poorest one-room hut had its ikon corner, where members of the family prayed regularly. Now, because these ikons showed Jesus, Mary, or one of the saints making the sign of the cross with only two fingers, Nikon declared them false. He confiscated them, had their painted eyes knocked out, and paraded their mutilated remains through the streets. The outrage against these and similar desecrations was so great that, in 1667, Tsar Alexis called a great church council to deal with the matter.

The council deposed Nikon as Patriarch, but upheld his reforms. It excommunicated at one stroke all those who refused to give up the old ritual, and thereby shattered the unity of the Russian Church. The "Old Believers" stood firm. They had not left the church, they said. The church had left the people. The Tsar, whom they had formerly revered as the only truly Christian monarch of the only truly Christian people, they now condemned as Antichrist. Wasn't his seal a double-headed eagle? And wasn't an eagle with two heads an unnatural monster?

The most fanatical of the Old Believers chose martyrdom by fire. A leading monk, Avvakum, who was burned at the stake, wrote from his prison cell, "Burning your body, you commend your soul to the hands of God." Entire communities of Old Believers shut themselves up in their wooden churches, put them to the torch, and perished in the flames. Literally thousands died in this way. Many others fled to the frontier to found religious colonies in the wilderness. Still others formed underground congregations in their towns or villages. The monks of the Solovetsky Monastery defied the council and openly resisted the troops sent to force their submission.

Religious dissent helped to ignite the greatest peasant rebellion yet known to Russian history. It was led by Stenka Razin, a Cossack of the Don region, who twice made pilgrimages of more than a thousand miles to the Solovetsky Monastery. Like the monks in the north, the Cossacks in the south represented the independent spirit of the frontier resisting the centralizing control of the Tsarist autocracy.

Stenka Razin's older brother had been fighting on the Russian side in the war against Poland when a dispute with the Russian generals prompted him to withdraw his Cossack force. He was accused of desertion, tried, and put to death. Young Stenka swore undying vengeance. He raised a band of outlaws, crossed to the lower Volga region, and spent two years as a river pirate and border raider on the Persian frontier.

In 1670, he appeared at the mouth of the Volga in command of a small army. At his call for class warfare, an oppressed people responded. Serfs butchered landlords. Townsmen murdered government officials. Runaways and renegades flocked to Razin's banner. Troops sent against him deserted to his side. Town after town surrendered. Razin's revolt spread up the Volga for more than a thousand miles; but as it approached the settled heartland of Muscovy, its strength waned. In the fall of 1670, Razin suffered his first defeat. In the following spring, he was captured and executed.

Razin had been dead for a year when the great bell announced the birth of the Tsarevich Peter in the Kremlin, but the echoes of his revolt still reverberated along the frontier. The hatred of serfs for landlords, of natives for "Germans," of Cossacks for the central government, and of Old Believers for the new ritual deeply divided the people of Muscovy. When young Peter came of age, he would have to cope with these antagonisms, but on the day of the procession that celebrated his birth, the division that most immediately threatened his future was not among his people or away on the frontier, but amid those who marched directly behind the Tsar. It was the division in the royal House of Romanov.

Chapter 2

A HOUSE DIVIDED

As a young man, Tsar Alexis had married Maria Miloslavsky. Their fourteen children had included five boys, all of them frail. One had died in infancy, and a second, at the age of four. In 1669, the Tsaritsa herself died in childbirth, and within a few months death struck again. This time the victim was the Tsarevich Alexis, the Tsar's sixteen-year-old son and heir apparent. The two remaining sons, Fyodor and Ivan, were so sickly that they were not expected to live to manhood. The House of Romanov was clearly in need of a healthy male heir, and at forty, Tsar Alexis announced that he would marry again.

The Tsar's principal minister and favorite was Artemon Matveyev. Matveyev was one of the most Europeanized Russians of his day, and his house contained many curiosities imported from the west. There were "German" paintings that gave a dizzying illusion of three-dimensionality, and a silvered mirror that reflected an image so clear and bright that Alexis could count every hair of his beard.

Yet nothing at Matveyev's was more of a novelty than his "German" wife, the daughter of a Scottish royalist in exile.

During the Mongol period, the Russians had adopted the oriental custom of segregating women of rank in separate living quarters called the terem. Life in the terem was deadly dull, and Matveyev's wife had escaped it. She moved freely among her male guests, enlivening the conversation and giving them a taste of mixed society as it was known in the west. Moreover, she permitted the same freedom to her husband's young ward and kinswoman, Natalia Naryshkin.

Natalia was a beautiful and lively young girl in her teens, and the moment Alexis laid eyes on her, he fell deeply in love. They were married in January, 1671, and in June of the following year, Natalia gave birth to the desired male heir. Little Peter was an exceptionally healthy baby and Alexis was overjoyed. In his gratitude for Peter's birth, the Tsar rewarded his wife's kin. Matveyev was raised to the rank of boyar, and Natalia's father was made a privy councillor.

While Natalia Naryshkin's family basked in the Tsar's favor, the kinsmen of his first wife were put in the shade. As long as Maria Miloslavsky had lived, Miloslavskys had enjoyed honor and influence. Now, while the Naryshkins occupied a central position at court, the Miloslavskys were pushed to one side. Ivan Miloslavsky, the head of the clan, was sent to serve on a distant frontier. It was almost like being in exile. But in an autocracy, fortunes often change with dramatic suddenness. In February, 1676, when Peter was only three, the normally robust Alexis was taken ill. Despite all his German doctors could do, he died in a few days.

He was succeeded by Peter's half brother, Fyodor.

Fyodor was both well-educated and good-hearted, but he was only fifteen, sickly, and was easily led. He soon fell under the influence of his wily uncle, Ivan Miloslavsky, who returned to the court. Ivan contrived the downfall of Matveyev by having him convicted of witchcraft. The mysterious symbols in a German algebra book found in his library were taken as evidence of black magic. He was sent into exile, and was soon followed by two of Natalia's brothers.

With her husband dead, her guardian in exile, and her family in disgrace, Natalia faced an altered world. With Peter's younger sister, Natasha, she occupied a modest apartment in the palace, but Peter continued to live the life traditional for a Tsarevich. There were four dwarfs among his attendants, and he had plenty of toys. The number of drums suggests that he was a boisterous child, fond of making noise.

At five, he was given a tutor. Nikita Zotov was a clerk in one of the government offices and no scholar, but he taught Peter the same sort of thing that had been taught to his father. Peter learned to read from the Bible, and to sing by note. Years later, Peter could quote whole passages of scripture by heart, and throughout his life he enjoyed singing with the church choir. Using elaborately illustrated picture books, Zotov told Peter stories of Russian heroes: Alexander Nevsky, who had destroyed the Swedes on the Neva River; Dimitry Donskoy, who had repulsed the Mongols on the Don; and Ivan the Terrible, who had conquered the Volga region from Kazan to Astrakhan. The boy learned to add and multiply after a fashion, but not to subtract or divide. His handwriting was poor, and his grammar and spelling remained erratic throughout his life.

While the young Tsarevich was getting this rudimentary education, a web of intrigue was being woven around his half brother Fyodor. The various personal and party alliances were constantly changing. To begin with, Ivan Miloslavsky and his family held the real power, and the Naryshkins were virtually helpless, but they had potential allies among the conservative aristocrats. Many of these had enjoyed honor and influence under Tsar Alexis, and they hated Ivan Miloslavsky because he treated them with insolence and contempt. In the end, both factions were outmaneuvered by a group known as "the young favorites." These last succeeded in weaning the gullible Fyodor away from his uncle, Ivan Miloslavsky, by persuading him to marry a young woman whom they controlled. Still, the situation was unstable, and no one could be sure what tomorrow would bring.

Amid all this uncertainty, one group held a position of strategic importance in Moscow. This was the Streltsy. *Streltsy* means literally "shooters," and originally they had been bowmen; but now they were armed with muskets, swords, and pikes. They were paid salaries and kept in existence in peace time, like a standing army. In Moscow, they served as a combination of palace guard, police force, and fire department. There were twenty regiments, numbering 20,000 men, in the city. They lived in their own quarter with their wives and families, and they were permitted to practice trades and handicrafts to supplement their pay. Since their sons generally entered the Streltsy on reaching manhood, they were a sort of hereditary class, having a strong sense of their rights and privileges. They were frequently at odds with the nobles who served as their officers, and many of these were members of the conservative aristocrats.

In July, 1681, Tsar Fyodor's first wife died in childbirth, but the "young favorites" soon persuaded the ailing Tsar to marry again. This time, their choice fell on Marfa Apraxin. Since she was the goddaughter of Matveyev, the match had political overtones. The bride-to-be begged Fyodor to recall Matveyev from exile, and he agreed. The prospect of the return of their leader revived the Naryshkins. They drew closer to the aristocrats, who were eager for a change. Their opportunity could not be far off. Everyone knew that Tsar Fyodor would not have long to live. When he died, the succession would have to be decided between his brother Ivan, the last son of Maria Miloslavsky, and Peter, the sole son of Natalia Naryshkin. The death of Fyodor would renew the power struggle between the two branches of the House of Romanov.

Chapter 3

THE STRELTSY RIOTS

Early in May, 1682, the news of the long-awaited death of Tsar Fyodor spread through the city. A great crowd began to assemble in the Kremlin. The huge fortress contained a dozen churches and monasteries, the residence of the Patriarch, scores of government offices, storehouses, stables, and living quarters for an army of courtiers, officials, servants, and soldiers, but this day the focus of all attention was the palace of the Tsar.

It rose above the Red Square like a dream castle. It was an architectural fantasy of contrasting shapes, colors, and textures. Walls of brick or cut stone alternated with rough-hewn timber. Soaring towers painted red, green, or blue were crowned with bronze or tin onion domes and glittering spires. Below them, the walls were intersected by a bewildering variety of carved and painted galleries, balconies, portals, and staircases. The greatest of these was the staircase leading up to the Red Balcony. It was guarded by

Streltsy in long caftans of red, green, or purple, and tall pointed caps trimmed with fox fur. They allowed none but the great to pass.

The magnates of church and state were arriving in gilded and painted carriages. Their mounted coachmen shouted, cursed, and slashed with their whips to clear a path through the common people. When they alighted, in their felt boots and flowing robes, they turned disdainfully from the wailing beggars and picked their way up the stairs to the Red Balcony, where they disappeared into the Great Hall.

The body of the dead Tsar lay in state. Facing him, his two brothers, Ivan and Peter, sat side by side. At sixteen, Ivan seemed pale and ill. He slouched in his chair, staring at the limp hands in his lap. The ten-year-old Peter was erect and flushed with health. His alert brown eyes continually looked about him. Behind him, in a section reserved for the women of the royal family, his mother sat with the princesses of the Miloslavsky faction. The Patriarch Yoachim headed a splendidly bearded and robed delegation of church dignitaries. As the ministers and magnates took turns in bending and solemnly kissing the hand of the dead Tsar in farewell, an occasional metallic clink was heard. Fearing an ambush by Ivan Miloslavsky, the members of the aristocratic party were wearing chain mail beneath their silks and brocades.

When the leave-taking ceremony was over, the Patriarch stepped forward. "Lords and nobles of Muscovy," he began in a sonorous bass voice. "Our beloved Tsar Fyodor has gone to his Heavenly Father. He leaves behind no son. He is survived by two brothers. Which one is to be the new Tsar—the Tsarevich Ivan or the Tsarevich Peter?"

There was a moment of silence before a gray-bearded boyar gave the answer all had been expecting.

"The question must be put to the representatives of the whole people."

Everyone knew that the crowd in the Red Square did not represent the whole people: it was drawn almost entirely from Moscow. But the election of the first Romanov Tsar had been confirmed by a crowd in the Red Square, and traditions were sacred. The Patriarch moved out to the balcony and repeated what he had said to the nobles and churchmen word for word.

"Which one shall be the new Tsar?" he called. "The Tsarevich Ivan?" There were shouts. "Or the Tsarevich Peter?" A great roar arose. Clearly, the majority was for Peter.

"So be it!" said the Patriarch. "Peter is the new Tsar of Muscovy. May God bless His Tsarish Majesty!"

At ten, Peter was too young to rule, and his mother would act as regent; but he was expected to participate in ceremonies. With his mother, he made his first public appearance as Tsar at Fyodor's funeral. The Tsar's religious role was important. Russian ritual was solemn. And this was an especially significant occasion.

High above the mourners, the domed ceiling floated like the vault of Heaven. Hundreds of flickering candles lit the pale enamel faces and brightly colored robes of the saints painted against the gold background of the ikon screen. Bearded priests swung smoking censers, and the perfumed air echoed with the chanting of the choir and the pealing of bells. It was an impressive ceremony, but it dragged on for hours, and Peter was only ten. He grew restless. He told his mother he was hungry. She hushed him, but the willful Peter was not to be hushed. He persisted, and Natalia did not know how to say "No" to her son. In the end, they left the cathedral before the service was half over.

The congregation was scandalized. That the Tsar should publicly insult the memory of his brother at his funeral was a thing unheard of. After the service, Tsaritsa Tatyana, the sister of Peter's father and the oldest member of the royal family, burst in on Natalia to scold her, but Natalia's cousin made matters worse.

"Let the dead lie there," he interrupted curtly. "His Majesty, Tsar Peter, is not dead, but alive, and his health must be looked after."

The cunning Ivan, head of the Miloslavsky faction, knew how to take advantage of such blunders. He shut himself up in his palace to invent and spread rumors that would show Peter's supporters in the worst possible light. In a city where the basic means of communication was word of mouth, it was easy to spread rumors of the most fantastic kind, and they were soon rampant among the Streltsy. It was said, for example, that the conservative aristocrats had bribed Tsar Fyodor's German doctors to poison him. Then they had contrived the election of Peter so that the Naryshkins could rule in his name. They planned to put to death any Streltsy who lodged complaints against their aristocratic officers.

This was a particularly telling point with the Streltsy. Many of their officers were corrupt. They had been withholding the pay they were supposed to distribute to their regiments, and the Streltsy had been demanding justice in a number of angry petitions. The Dutch envoy wrote,

"Great calamities are feared, and not without cause, for the might of the Streltsy is great and redoubtable, and no resistance can be opposed to them."

The long-awaited return of Matveyev from exile was reassuring. He was experienced, wise, and universally respected. Even the Streltsy remembered him as a beloved former commander. But his ability was soon put to a crucial test.

On the morning of May 25, the Streltsy attended mass as usual, and although their officers had not ordered it, they were fully armed. After church, they stood about or drank in the taverns, conversing in low tones, as if they expected something. At nine o'clock, it came. A horseman galloped through the streets.

"To arms!" he shouted. "The Naryshkins have murdered the Tsarevich Ivan. To the palace! Death to the traitors!"

Instantly, the Streltsy formed ranks and marched toward the Kremlin with drums beating and banners flying. Too late, Matveyev got word of their coming. Before he could order the gates closed, the Streltsy were streaming across the Red Square. Ministers and boyars hurried to the Great Hall, where they found Matveyev, the Patriarch, and the royal family.

Matveyev decided that Tsarevich Ivan must be shown to the Streltsy to prove that he had not been murdered. Holding Ivan and Peter by the hand, Tsaritsa Natalia followed Matveyev, the Patriarch, and a group of boyars out onto the balcony. At the sight of them, a roar went up from ten thousand throats. The square was a sea of tossing caps, fluttering banners, and gleaming pikes.

The Patriarch stepped to the railing. "Here is the Tsar Peter," he called in the melodious tones in which he chanted Mass. "Here is the Tsaritsa Natalia, widow of Tsar Alexis, blessed of memory. Here is the Tsarevich Ivan. See for yourselves that all are alive and well. Thank merciful God for the good health of the royal family."

A confused muttering ran through the crowd. Many of the Streltsy were drunk, and even the powerful voice of the Patriarch could not be heard by all. There was a sudden stir below. Half a dozen fire ladders were thrown up to the balcony railing. A moment later, tall pointed caps, fierce bright eyes, and bristling beards rose into view only a few feet from where the royal family stood.

"Where is the Tsarevich Ivan?" one of them bawled.

"Here," said Matveyev, putting an arm around the frail youth. The Streltsy stared from atop their ladders. Then all began to talk at once.

"Are you the Tsarevich Ivan? . . . They haven't killed you after all? . . . Are you really he?"

At that moment, the Streltsy at the foot of the staircase burst through the gate and swarmed up the steps like a red, green, and purple wave. At the top they paused, flushed with heat, excitement, and vodka.

"Here is the Tsarevich Ivan," Matveyev called out. "He has come to no harm and will come to none."

"It is the Tsarevich Ivan," one of the Streltsy called back over his shoulder. Others took up the cry below. Matveyev stepped close to the railing and raised his arms for silence.

"My old comrades-in-arms," he began, "I once had the honor to serve our beloved Tsar as your commander. Together we fought for the glory of Muscovy, the Orthodox Tsar, and the One True Faith."

As the Streltsy fell silent, Matveyev motioned to Natalia

to take Peter and Ivan inside. From the Great Hall, they could hear the old minister skillfully soothing and flattering the crowd. He praised the Streltsy for their past services and their loyal concern for the safety of the royal family. He assured them that all would be well. They could rely on a sympathetic hearing of all their grievances. They had his word that the new Tsar would deal justly and generously with the brave soldiers who had served his father and brother so heroically.

When Matveyev bade them farewell and stepped back inside, the Streltsy began to disperse. Unfortunately, one of their hated boyar commanders tried to speed them on their way with orders barked in an imperious and insulting tone. His words were so many sparks, rekindling all their pent-up rage. In a sudden rush a group of soldiers seized the boyar and hurled him over the balcony onto the up-raised pikes of their comrades below. The Streltsy riots had begun.

A mob burst through the doorway to the Great Hall. With a scream Natalia flung her arms around Matveyev. Before Peter's eyes, the old man was torn from her grasp and carried out. The soldiers swung him in a high arc. For a moment, his twisted body, gray beard, and disheveled robes seemed to freeze in silhouette against the blue of the sky. Then he plummeted out of sight.

The palace echoed with thudding footsteps, the whoops of the hunters, and the screams of the victims. A boyar was cut down in the mistaken belief that he was Natalia's brother Ivan Naryshkin. Another brother was pulled from under the altar in a chapel and hacked to pieces. Half a dozen other boyars and ministers were tracked down and killed. At night the Streltsy withdrew, but those who had escaped detection by hiding in the bedroom of Peter's little sister could not get out of the Kremlin past the Streltsy guards.

The riots lasted three days. Government offices were looted and records destroyed. New victims were searched out and killed, but Natalia's brother, Ivan Naryshkin, continued to elude capture. In the end, Peter's older half sister Sophia convinced Natalia that the only way to save them all from death was to surrender Ivan. Natalia went to her brother's hiding place and explained. Accepting his fate courageously, Ivan took Holy Communion and, with an ikon of the Virgin in his hand, walked out of the gates of the palace. The Streltsy showed no mercy. They dragged him away, put him to torture, and hacked his body to pieces. This satisfied them at last, and the bloodshed ceased.

It is probable that Peter was never in real danger. The blood lust of the Streltsy was keen, but not indiscriminate. They hated only those they thought they had reason to hate. Peter and his mother were blameless in their eyes, but Peter could not have known this. The horrors of those days haunted his dreams, convulsed his nervous system, and made the Kremlin hideous to him from that time forth. He was never again able to sleep without a companion in his room. The Streltsy riots would echo in Peter's mind until the day of his death.

Chapter **4**

THE EMERGENCE OF SOPHIA

"She is immensely fat with a head as large as a bushel, hairs on her face, and tumors on her legs . . . , but in the same degree that her stature is short, broad, and coarse, her mind is shrewd, unprejudiced, and full of policy." The words describe Peter's half sister Sophia as she appeared to the French ambassador a few years later. At the time of the Streltsy riots, she was only twenty-five, but she was already showing the mental qualities the Frenchman admired.

Along with her brother Fyodor, she had been tutored by a monk who knew French, Latin, and the culture of the west. In the Muscovy of her day, such an education was exceptional even for a man. It was unique for a woman. Besides her fine mind, Sophia possessed all the strength of will and physical vitality Fyodor lacked. During his frequent illnesses, she had taken advantage of their kinship to stay at his bedside and relay his orders to his ministers.

In this way, she had developed a real grasp of government and a habit of command. She had also come to know and fall passionately in love with a remarkable boyar, Prince Vasily Golitsyn.

Sophia and the Prince made a curious pair. She was gifted with none of the comeliness and physical grace he had in abundance. Perhaps he made love to her only to advance his political ambitions, but he genuinely admired her intelligence, her strength, and her enthusiasm for the west.

The supporters of Peter were demoralized. The death of Matveyev had deprived them of a leader. The male Naryshkins were either murdered or in hiding. Peter's mother, Natalia, was bewildered and inexperienced. There was a power vacuum in the Kremlin, and with the help of her uncle, Ivan Miloslavsky, Sophia was quick to occupy it. Vasily Golitsyn took charge of foreign affairs. Ivan Miloslavsky assumed control of several other departments. Most important of all, their ally, Prince Khovansky, became the new commander of the Streltsy.

Working through Khovansky, the Miloslavsky faction manipulated the Streltsy cleverly. They agreed to pay ten rubles per man as compensation for back pay. They courted them with drink and played on the injustice of passing over Tsarevich Ivan in favor of the much younger Peter. On June 3, Khovansky brought to the palace a Streltsy demand that the Tsarevich Ivan be raised to the throne jointly with his brother. Under the threat of force, the council called to consider the matter had no real choice. A dual monarchy was proclaimed. Soon afterward, a delegation of Streltsy requested that Sophia replace Natalia as regent for the two brothers. Again a council was called, and again the result was a foregone conclusion. Sophia was declared Regent and assumed authority in name as well as in fact.

The coronation of the Tsars was scheduled for July 5. Peter and Ivan shared their father's throne. It was divided down the middle by a handsome silver bar symbolizing the division of the royal family into two factions. Still more revealing was the hole in the back through which an unseen prompter could whisper to the young Tsars what they were supposed to say and do. The brothers were not so much rivals as the twin puppets of the sister who held the power behind the throne.

Immediately after the coronation, Sophia had to deal with the first challenge to her regency. The Streltsy included a number of Old Believers, and since Khovansky was one himself, he encouraged his men to petition Sophia for a return to the old ritual. Following a disorderly debate in the Great Hall, Sophia invited the Streltsy in groups of a hundred at a time to banquets at the palace, where she personally handed round wine and vodka. With a combination of gifts, promises, honeyed words, and strong drink, she gradually won their loyalty. As a result, when a monk who was the chief spokesman for the Old Believers appeared in the Streltsy quarter to agitate for the cause, they seized him and delivered him to Sophia. She promptly had him beheaded.

Open dissent was crushed, but it was clear to Sophia that Khovansky was not to be trusted. As long as she remained in Moscow, she was at his mercy. The Kremlin was a prison to which his Streltsy held the key. Her only hope lay in escape. Toward the end of July, without advance warning, she, the two Tsars, and the remainder of the royal family slipped out of Moscow for the summer palace of Kolomenskoe. To allay suspicion she explained that she had wished to get away from the heat of the capital.

A few weeks later, Sophia began to move again. The pretext was a series of pilgrimages to various monasteries, but they were so arranged that each move took the court farther from Moscow and closer to the monastery of Troitsa. Once inside its towering walls, forty miles from Moscow, she would be safe from attack. Even during the course of the journey, her strength grew. A Streltsy regiment acting as escort was already loyal to her. She could count on the support of the rural nobility to raise an army. The size of her court was constantly increasing. In Russia, the celebration of the day dedicated to the saint for whom a baby is named is as great an occasion as a birthday in the west, and Sophia used the celebration of her name day to invite most of the principal nobles and officials of Moscow to her side.

She now felt strong enough to strike. On the morning of her name day she called a council of magnates, at which she accused Khovansky of plotting to seize the throne. The council found him guilty and condemned him to death. He was beheaded the following day.

When the news reached Moscow, the Streltsy expected an attack and immediately occupied the Kremlin, but Sophia saw no need for further bloodshed. She called on the Streltsy to offer submission, and ultimately they gave in. Sophia then appointed a loyal follower named Shaklovity to be their new commander, and late in November, she led the royal family back to the capital in triumph.

It is unlikely that the ten-year-old Peter understood his sister's maneuvers, but there is little doubt that he enjoyed

the months in the country. He was fond of travel, and the
return to the Kremlin was disagreeable, but he did not have
to remain there. Sophia now held the reins of power so
firmly that she no longer required the presence of both
Tsars to bolster her authority. Early in 1683, she permitted
Peter, his mother, and his sister Natasha to leave the hated
confines of the Kremlin and move into the wooden summer
palace of Preobrazhensky.

Chapter **5**

PALACE CEREMONIES
AND BOYHOOD GAMES

Preobrazhensky was only three miles from the Kremlin, and as a crowned Tsar, Peter had to return to the Great Hall of the palace from time to time to take part in ceremonies and grant audiences along with his brother Ivan. It was customary for new rulers to confirm the treaties made by their predecessors. For this purpose, the boy Tsars received a series of embassies.

A delegate with the Swedish mission described Peter at the age of eleven. Both Tsars wore robes of silver woven with red-and-white flowers. Their caps, robes, and long golden staffs glittered with diamonds, emeralds, and other precious stones. Peter was so large for his age that the writer mistook him for sixteen. He had "a frank and open face." His "great beauty and lively manner" contrasted with the simpleminded Ivan's dullness and dejection. When it came time to ask the ceremonial questions, Ivan "hindered the proceedings through not understanding what was going on," while Peter jumped up and "had to be pulled back until the elder brother had a chance of speaking."

The next year, a Saxon doctor described Peter as friendly, gracious, and remarkably good-looking. He had "a beauty that gains the heart of all who see him and a mind which, even in its early years, did not find its like." The Dutch minister was equally flattering. "His stature is great, and his mien is fine. . . . He grows visibly and advances as much in intelligence and understanding." He showed "such a strong preference for military pursuits that, when he comes of age, we may surely expect from him brave actions and heroic deeds."

In Preobrazhensky, Peter was playing soldier with energy and enthusiasm. This was no game with toys. His attendants served as live soldiers. They were dressed in uniforms and equipped with weapons sent from the Kremlin. After his eleventh birthday, he was permitted real brass cannon, and a German artillery officer showed him how to fire salutes. He ordered drummer boys and became an expert drummer himself. He expanded his forces into a full regiment and then two. He recruited the sons of great boyars along with youths of humble origin, and he employed "German" officers to train his companions in western military methods.

Peter and his friends referred to the regiments as "the Guards," but in Moscow, they were called "the amusement grooms." Peter's father, Tsar Alexis, had been an avid hunter and had employed hundreds of grooms and huntsmen for the purpose. It was natural for people to think of Peter's play regiments as only another variety of royal amusement. No one took them seriously. General Patrick Gordon, a Scot in the Muscovite service who would later become one of Peter's most trusted generals, mentioned Peter's marches condescendingly as "military ballets."

Yet the games were a healthy outlet for Peter's abundant energy. Instead of assuming personal command, he took the title of Bombardier and shared fully in the life of his comrades. He ate the same food, lived in the same quarters, and marched in the ranks on expeditions that ranged as far as the Troitsa Monastery, forty miles away. He loved the rough life of the camp. It developed him physically, and sharing the same hut or tent with his comrades at night eased the nightmares that had haunted him since the Streltsy riots.

Preobrazhensky means "transformation" or "transfiguration," and during the years there, Peter developed an attitude radically different from that of his ancestors. The view from the camp at Preobrazhensky was far broader than from the Great Hall of the Kremlin. The life style of Peter's formative years was in sharp contrast to the slow-moving ritual that governed the daily routine of earlier Tsars. He took to wearing clothes that offered his restless body freedom of movement and came to hate his ceremonial vestments. His appetite was always ravenous, and he learned to eat peasant food with peasant manners, using his fingers more often than not. He craved physical activity and avoided the confinement of the court whenever he could.

He had a talent for working with his hands. His powerful physique was an asset at the forge and anvil, and he was as dexterous as he was strong. He became expert with the turning lathe. He learned to operate a printing press and to bind books. Instinctively, he tried his hand at every skill that came to his attention, and was not satisfied until he had mastered it. His early education had lacked discipline, but his extraordinary curiosity led him to return to his studies with new energy.

He heard that in Europe they had an instrument that could measure distances from far away, and he asked Prince Dolgoruky, who was about to leave on an embassy to Paris, to bring him one of these wonderful devices. The Prince agreed, and in May, 1688, shortly before Peter's sixteenth birthday, he returned with an astrolabe. The youthful Tsar was delighted by the gleaming finish of its metal and the precision of the craftmanship, but when he asked Dolgoruky how it worked, the Prince was at a loss. The question had never even occurred to him.

Peter's inquiries led him to a Dutch merchant, Timmermann, who was reported to have a knowledge of such things. At the Tsar's request, Timmermann sighted through the astrolabe and made some calculations. When he had estimated the distance to a neighboring house, a soldier was sent to pace it off. The two measurements checked precisely. Delighted, Peter asked the Dutchman to show him how it worked. Timmermann answered that Peter would have to learn arithmetic and trigonometry first.

He agreed, and the two set to work. Their copy books still exist. The problems are written in Timmermann's hand. They are followed by Peter's awkward attempts to work the solutions. The figures are crude, and there are many mistakes, but successive copy books show steady improvement.

The astrolabe was only the opening wedge. It introduced him to mathematics useful for the understanding of gunnery and fortification. These in turn required some knowledge of physics. The mathematical measurement of distances was part of mapmaking and geography. Peter got out his globe. Geography awakened his interest in astronomy, and so it went. The arrival of the astrolabe launched him on a process of self-education that would be lifelong.

A month later, Peter made another discovery. He and some friends were poking about in the barn of an estate he had inherited from a relative, Nikita Romanov. In a corner, they found a curious boat. Instead of being flat-bottomed like Russian boats, it had a keel. It was an English boat and may have been a gift from Queen Elizabeth to Ivan the Terrible. Timmermann said that such boats could sail against the wind. Peter wanted to put it in the water at once, but it required repairing first. Fortunately, there was living in the German Suburb an old Dutch shipwright named Karsten Brandt, brought to Russia by Peter's father. Brandt was sent for, and while Peter watched in fascination, the old man caulked the seams, tarred the hull, and fitted the little boat with a mast and sail. Then, launching it in the Yauza River, Brandt showed the young Tsar how to tack against the wind. "And mighty pleasant it was to me," Peter wrote many years later.

His pleasure soon gave way to discontent. Once he had the knack of sailing, the river was too narrow for his liking. A nearby pond proved little better. He heard that there was a fine large lake at Peryaslavl, but it was fifty miles beyond the Troitsa Monastery, and it would be hard to get his mother's permission to travel so far. Instead of telling her his real destination, he asked to attend a religious festival at the monastery. When it was over, he drove the remaining distance to Peryaslavl.

The lake was splendid. Its glittering waters spread out nearly as far as his eyes could see. Rather than bring the

little boat nearly a hundred miles from Preobrazhensky, he
suggested to Brandt that they build a larger and better
ship right there. Brandt was agreeable, but once again, the
Tsaritsa's consent was an obstacle. At first she refused, but
Peter pleaded so persistently that she gave in, provided he
would wait for the celebration of his name day on July 9.
On July 10, he set off with Brandt and several companions
for his first attempt at shipbuilding.

Chapter **6**

CONFRONTATION

At sixteen, Peter had spent five years doing almost as he pleased. He genuinely loved his mother, and at her request he would put off his own pleasures long enough to attend a court ceremony or a special mass, but he was too impetuous and self-willed to be domesticated. In view of the freedom he enjoyed, it is remarkable that his pastimes should have been as constructive as they were. Purely by choice, he practiced mechanical and military skills, studied mathematics and geometry, learned to sail and build ships. On the other hand, he took no interest in the business of the state, and began to show a weakness for drinking with "Germans" and other low companions. When he returned from Peryaslavl in September, 1688, Natalia thought it was high time for her prodigal son to settle down.

Peter was the natural focal point of renewed opposition to the Miloslavskys. Ivan Miloslavsky had died, leaving Sophia the undisputed leader of her party. Natalia's brother Lev headed the Naryshkin faction. But the power struggle extended far beyond the two branches of the royal family. Conservative aristocrats like Prince Boris Golitsyn and Patriarch Yoachim opposed Sophia for the very qualities westerners admired. They thought a woman's place was in the terem, and their hatred of all things "German" made them even more hostile to her lover, Prince Vasily Golitsyn.

Although he was a boyar, a Golitsyn, and a cousin of the conservative Boris, Prince Vasily's way of life and outlook were remarkably western. He shaved like a German and wore German clothes. His residence reminded the French ambassador of the palace of a great Italian prince. He spoke Latin fluently. His ideas for the development of trade, the reform of the army, and the possible emancipation of the serfs marked him as one of the most progressive Russians of his time.

Since Peter was himself an admirer of the west, it is ironic that the conservatives should have backed him to oppose the westernizing tendencies of Sophia and her lover. But they did not know Peter. To them, he was simply a precocious and eccentric boy wholly indifferent to politics. As long as they allowed him to amuse himself with his queer games, they could count on him to leave the actual government to them. By contrast, Sophia was clearly eager to rule in her own right. Although her simpleminded brother Ivan had come of age, she showed no sign of relinquishing power. Instead, she had begun to use the title of "Autocrat" on state documents. According to some, she had even inspired an abortive attempt to persuade the Streltsy to petition for her coronation.

As long as her regency was successful, the conservative opposition was weak, but, in 1687, Sophia suffered her first setback. In alliance with Poland, Austria, and Venice,

Muscovy declared war on Turkey, and Prince Vasily led an army into the Crimea. The taxes for the war were unpopular. The campaign was a disaster. Without once engaging the enemy in a battle, Prince Vasily lost 40,000 men to disease, hardship, and guerilla action. Just before Peter's return from Peryaslavl, Sophia announced that there would be a second campaign the following spring. The conservatives were incensed. The Patriarch prophesied that only disaster could befall an army in which Catholic heretics like Gordon were permitted to command soldiers of the One True Faith.

Peter had other interests. Two months at Peryaslavl with Brandt and Timmermann had improved his Dutch, and he was beginning to show a lively pleasure in the young ladies of the German Suburb. Natalia disapproved. She felt it was high time for her son to marry. Going on seventeen, he was nearly seven feet tall and physically mature for his age. A wife would help to steady him emotionally. She would keep him at home to attend to the business of the court. Besides, there was the succession to think of. Peter's half brother Ivan had been married for four years, but had had only daughters. If Peter could produce a male heir, it would strengthen his claim to the throne. Lev Naryshkin, Boris Golitsyn, and other conservatives agreed.

Peter had no desire for marriage and consented only to please his mother. He left the choice of his future wife entirely to Natalia and her advisers. The bride they chose was Eudoxia Lopukhin, the daughter of a boyar well connected with the conservatives. Three years older than Peter, she had been brought up in the confinement of the terem, and her imagination had not ventured beyond its walls. She was pretty, timid, dull, and conventional in the extreme. A worse match for the restless, impulsive, and impatient young Tsar would have been hard to find.

The wedding was celebrated in the old way on February 6, 1689. Eudoxia was heavily rouged and painted. A close-fitting pearl-studded cap hid her hair. Her braids were pulled so tight that she could scarcely blink her eyes. A high stiff collar circled her throat. Layers of petticoats, silk, and brocade enveloped the rest of her body. After the lively and buxom beauties of the German Suburb, she seemed less a woman than a life-sized Muscovite doll.

The ceremony was heavy with traditional symbolism. At one point, Eudoxia's father took a plaited leather whip from his belt and struck her across the back three times so hard that she winced. Then he presented the whip to Peter as a token that he was her new lord and master. If she failed to please him, he was entitled to beat her.

As might have been expected, Eudoxia did fail to please him, but instead of beating her, Peter ignored her. Two months after the wedding, he left for Peryaslavl, where he wrote, not to his bride, but to his mother. "I ask thy blessing and desire about thy health, and we, through thy prayers, are all well, and the lake is all got clear from the ice today, and all the boats except the big one are finished. Only we are waiting for rope, and therefore I beg your kindness that these ropes, seven hundred fathoms long, be sent from the Artillery Department without delay, for the work is waiting for them, and our sojourn here is being prolonged. For this I ask your blessing."

The letter was written on a dirty scrap of paper in a scrawl that trembled as if the hand that held the pen had only just laid down an ax. It angered Natalia. Instead of sending the rope, she ordered him to return for a memorial mass for Tsar Fyodor on the anniversary of his death. The situation in the capital was tense. The Dutch envoy wrote to Holland: "If the campaign against the Tartars shall be no more successful than the last, there will probably be a general rebellion." But at Peryaslavl, Peter thought of nothing but his ships. He wrote his mother, "As to what thou hast done in ordering me to go to Moscow, I am ready, only hey! hey! there is work here."

A second summons from Natalia brought Peter to Moscow in time for the mass, but a month later he was back at Peryaslavl. This time he was able to sail one of the completed ships. In a jubilant letter, he compared himself to Noah and signed himself "Petrus" in the Latin rather than the Russian alphabet. He did not write Eudoxia, or even mention her in his letters. His response to a personal messenger whom Natalia sent to urge his return to Moscow showed careless unconcern. "Hey! I wish to hear about thy health and beg thy blessing. We are all well, and about the boats, I say again they are mighty good."

But Peter could not put off his responsibilities forever, and when he returned to the capital early in July, his supporters finally convinced him that Sophia planned to seize the throne. She must be checked, and checked soon. July 18 was the Festival of the Miraculous Appearance of the Virgin of Kazan. As usual, mass was celebrated in the Cathedral of the Assumption before the procession to the Cathedral of Kazan. As usual, both Sophia and her two brothers took part. When the mass was over and as the procession was forming, Peter approached Sophia. At nearly seven feet, he towered over her like a young wolf over a bulldog. His handsome and still-beardless cheeks were flushed with embarrassment and determination. Sophia raised her broad face calmly and waited. The gentle half-wit Ivan smiled uncertainly from one to the other. Peter's jaw worked convulsively. When he spoke at last, his hoarse deep voice carried clearly to the courtiers who ringed them in the dim light of the cathedral.

"As crowned Tsar of All the Russias," he said, "I forbid you to march in this procession."

Sophia stared. Muscovite tradition kept the women of the royal family inconspicuous. During religious processions, they were screened from view behind canopies. Sophia had broken with custom to emerge into the public eye. If she now obeyed Peter's command and returned to the obscurity of the terem, her right to participate in any affair of state would end. Peter was really challenging her right to rule.

Sophia was equal to the occasion. Without a word, she turned and took the sacred ikon of the Virgin. Then she marched slowly and deliberately after the bearded priests leading the procession.

Peter stood watching helplessly. The flush on his face deepened. Then he turned on his heel and strode rapidly in the opposite direction.

Chapter 7

THE FLIGHT TO TROITSA

Before the procession had reached the Cathedral of Kazan, Peter was galloping out of Moscow. A long lull followed. Rumors spread and suspicion simmered, but neither side dared open conflict. Peter's party was too weak to attack Sophia in the Kremlin. Sophia refrained from ordering the Streltsy against Preobrazhensky.

The commander of the Streltsy, Shaklovity, took elaborate precautions to safeguard Sophia. On Peter's side, Lev Naryshkin bribed spies among the Streltsy to inform him of developments in the Kremlin. As the tension mounted, Sophia and Shaklovity courted Streltsy loyalty with inflammatory speeches against Peter's supporters. To a few leaders, Shaklovity even suggested disposing of Peter's advisers, Lev Naryshkin and Boris Golitsyn, and putting Natalia into a convent.

Early in August, 1689, Sophia requested an escort of Streltsy for a pilgrimage into the country. Shaklovity mobilized a far larger force than necessary. The main body was stationed inside the Kremlin, but smaller detachments were posted in the Kitaygorod and even outside the city walls toward Preobrazhensky. This gave rise to new rumors. Many Streltsy believed that they were preparing to attack. Toward midnight, Peter's spies heard a report that the signal to march had been given. They galloped at full speed to warn the young Tsar.

Roused from a sound sleep, Peter was told that the Streltsy were advancing from the Kremlin, three miles away. There was not a moment to lose. In bare feet and wearing only a shirt, he flung himself on a horse and rode into a wood to wait for an escort with his clothes. When it arrived, he dressed and continued his flight. The little band rode through the night, through the sunrise, and through the early morning. At about six, they came in sight of the gleaming walls of the Troitsa Monastery. This was the rendezvous Lev Naryshkin and Boris Golitsyn had planned in case of emergency. Peter was now safe, but he had ridden forty miles in fear of his life, and he burst into tears as he told the Abbot of Sophia's treachery.

In the Kremlin, there was no awareness of all this. Not until Sophia had attended morning mass did she get word that her half brother had galloped off into the night clad only in a shirt. Shaklovity concluded that he had gone mad. But if Peter had been temporarily deranged by fear, the plan he was following was anything but mad. Safe inside the Troitsa Monastery, he could now adopt the strategy Sophia had used so effectively against Khovansky seven years before.

Within a few hours, Peter was joined by many supporters. His mother, his sister, and his newly pregnant wife were there along with Lev Naryshkin, Boris Golitsyn, and other conservative leaders. The Guards arrived. Still more reassuring was the appearance of a regiment of Streltsy loyal to Peter's cause.

After conferring with his advisers, the young Tsar sent to Sophia to ask why there were so many armed Streltsy in the Kremlin. Her answer that they were intended only as an escort for a pilgrimage convinced no one. New arrivals from Moscow attributed various evil designs to Sophia and Shaklovity. For several days, messengers and delegations moved back and forth. There were orders and counterorders. Peter demanded representatives of the Streltsy to report to him. Sophia ordered them to remain. It was as if the Kremlin and the Troitsa Monastery contained huge opposing magnets. But while Peter's pull grew stronger, Sophia's steadily weakened. Increasing numbers of Streltsy left Moscow for the Troitsa Monastery, and when Sophia sent the Patriarch to plead her case, he defected to the conservative aristocrats.

On September 8, Sophia decided that she must go to the Troitsa Monastery herself. With Vasily Golitsyn, Shaklovity, and a Streltsy escort, she set out, but in the same village where she had beheaded Khovansky seven years before, she was intercepted by an order from Peter that she return to Moscow at once. She could do nothing but obey. Next, Peter demanded that she surrender Shaklovity. She flatly refused, but her authority was waning. The foreign officers in the German Suburb rode off to join Peter. Crowds appeared in the Red Square calling for the surrender of Shaklovity. In the end, Sophia was forced to do with Shaklovity what she had forced Natalia to do with her brother during the Streltsy riots. On September 17, Shaklovity took Holy Communion and set off for the

Troitsa Monastery. At the same time, Prince Vasily slipped quietly out of Moscow and deserted his former mistress for a villa in the country.

At the Troitsa Monastery, Shaklovity was examined under torture. This was standard procedure for such cases. For centuries, trial by torture had been the common practice throughout Europe and would continue in every state on the continent well into the eighteenth century. There was a kind of perverted logic to justify it. After all, who was a more convincing witness than the accused? What was more authentic evidence than his personal confession? And what was a more persuasive means of extracting such confession than torture?

Peter was sitting with Lev Naryshkin and Boris Golitsyn when Shaklovity was brought in. The scribe appointed to record the answers to their questions sharpened a quill pen. The candles of his writing desk made the only pool of light in the dungeon gloom. The commander of the Streltsy was stripped to the waist and his hands tied behind his back. A block of stone was fixed to his ankles, and a rope attached to his wrists was passed across an overhead beam. When two soldiers pulled on this rope, the prisoner's wrists rose behind his back. At shoulder level, they began to tremble. Then, with a sickening crackle, the old man's shoulders turned inside out, and he hung helplessly with arms straight over his head.

Prince Boris Golitsyn asked the first question. "Is it true that you once suggested to your officers that they might petition for the coronation of Tsarevna Sophia?"

Shaklovity shook his head. The Prince gave a sign to the knoutmaster, who held a whip with a wooden handle fixed to a thick leather thong two feet long. Raising it in both hands, he sprang forward and brought it down with a whistling crack. It left a vertical stripe as thick as a man's finger from shoulder to waist beginning to ooze blood. Many questions and many strokes of the knout later, when the old man was finally cut down, his back was a crimson pulp, and his carefully recorded confession amounted to treason.

Four days later, Shaklovity and three accomplices were beheaded. Three others had their tongues torn out and were sent into exile. Thanks to the intervention of his cousin Boris, Prince Vasily Golitsyn was spared torture, but was banished for life to the province of Archangel. By the standards of the day, these punishments were not cruel, and many of Peter's party objected that they were too lenient.

Sophia was confined to a convent for life. She was permitted visits only from kinswomen and only on holy days, but her apartment had twelve well-furnished rooms, and she was given a number of servants. Life in the convent would not be much more confining than her years in the terem. But if Peter's punishment of Sophia was mild, his feelings were not. He hated her bitterly and refused to budge from the Troitsa Monastery until he had word that she was safely locked up.

He had no such hatred for his half brother. Peter was fond of Ivan and never thought of deposing him. He wrote from the Troitsa Monastery that now they would begin to rule as joint sovereigns without the interference of their sister. On his return to Moscow he went directly to Ivan, embraced him affectionately, and drew him out onto the

Red Balcony to receive the ovation of the cheering crowd. Yet it was obvious to everyone that the brothers were joint sovereigns in name only. Peter had been a puppet Tsar for seven years. Now his real reign could begin.

BOOK TWO

The Education of a Tsar

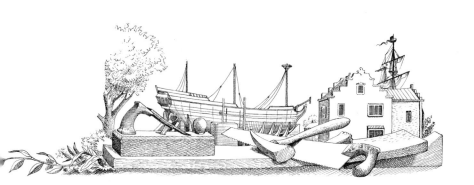

Chapter **8**

THE GERMAN SUBURB

Peter's reign began with a paradox. The three Romanov Tsars before him had come to the throne at sixteen, and had taken their duties seriously. He was seventeen, but he had no interest in government, and he left the administration of affairs entirely to conservative aristocrats. Therefore, the reign of Peter, the great westernizer, began with a fanatical attack on westerners.

The spearhead of this attack was the Patriarch Yoachim. With his flowing white beard and piercing eyes, he resembled an Old Testament prophet, and he burned with hatred for the foreign heretics gnawing at the core of Orthodox Muscovy. He obtained a decree that banished all Jesuits from the country within two weeks. Even before Peter returned from the Troitsa Monastery, where he was enjoying the company of Gordon and the other foreign officers, three Germans were sentenced to death for heresy in Moscow.

The borders were closed. Foreign travelers were detained

at the frontier until special orders from the Kremlin author-
ized them to enter the country. Mail from Europe was
opened and inspected. A number of letters, especially from
Catholic Poland, were confiscated and burned. The Patriarch and the conservative leaders were building a seventeenth-century version of the Iron Curtain around Russia.
But there was one important foreign influence that could
not be stopped at the frontier, because it was already established in the heart of Muscovy. This was the German
Suburb.

In 1652, Tsar Alexis had decreed that all "Germans"
must live in a special quarter outside the walls of Moscow.
There the westerners built what amounted to a little German city on the banks of the Yauza River, close to both
Moscow and Preobrazhensky. Its population was about ten
thousand. Germans and Poles predominated, but there
were many Swedes, Danes, Dutchmen, Englishmen, and
Scots, along with a sprinkling of Frenchmen and Italians.
Most of them were soldiers of fortune, but there were also
merchants, diplomats, physicians, apothecaries, and artisans of every kind. The Protestants had their own churches.
Catholics were forbidden to have a building, but even after
the expulsion of the Jesuits, they were allowed a priest who
celebrated mass in their private houses. The inhabitants intermarried, had children, and educated them on the western
pattern. They spoke western languages, read western periodicals, and, despite occasional problems with censorship, cor-
responded with friends and relatives in western Europe.

Their houses were better built than those in Moscow.
They left no rough timbers exposed, but stuccoed them
over or planed them smooth and sometimes painted them
to resemble bricks. They had gay window boxes and raised

strange flowers, such as the garden roses imported from Denmark. Their yards were free of the slops and garbage one saw in the city. They took care to lay out their gardens in neat geometric patterns with paths and clipped hedges. Tables and chairs were placed beneath fruit and shade trees.

The men seated around these tables did not wear long caftans and flowing beards like the Russians. Their tailored coats, knee breeches, and stockings showed the contours of their legs and bodies. Their shaven faces and trimmed hair scandalized Orthodox Russians, who regarded their

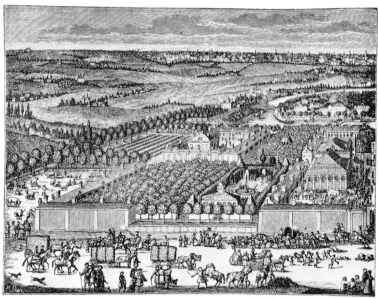

The German Suburb was like a little piece of western Europe transplanted in the heart of Muscovy. The large building in the center is the palace Peter presented to his favorite, Lefort. It was the scene of many huge banquets. Moscow is visible in the distance.

beards as sacred. It was true that a few aristocrats like Vasily Golitsyn wore German clothes and shaved, but this was rare. The year before his death, Tsar Alexis had strictly forbidden such customs. The beardless Germans smoked long-stemmed pipes of tobacco, known to Russians as "bewitched grass" or "devil's incense." Tsar Mikhail, Peter's grandfather, had outlawed smoking, and Tsar Alexis had considered making it punishable with death.

It is not certain when Peter first strayed into this strange forbidden city. He was sixteen when Timmermann taught him the use of the astrolabe and Brandt showed him how to sail. Around the same time, Gordon began to teach him to make fireworks, and there were a number of other residents it would have been natural for him to visit. The German Suburb was closer to Preobrazhensky than the Kremlin, and far more appealing. There was little to interest Peter in Moscow. His mother surrounded herself with old priests and monks who bored him, and Eudoxia's advancing pregnancy made her duller than ever.

In February, 1690, Eudoxia gave birth to a boy, Alexis, named for Peter's father. The arrival of a male heir occasioned great rejoicing in the capital, and Peter was pleased in his own way, but it is characteristic that he was more interested in the celebration than in the baby who caused it. With Gordon's help, he arranged an elaborate fireworks display, the first ever held in Moscow. It lasted more than five hours, and even though one of the five-pound rockets went astray and "carried off the head of a boyar," it was a great success.

At least one member of the court did not applaud. The Patriarch was well aware that the detested Catholic, Gordon, was behind Peter's knowledge of fireworks. When

Peter invited the Scot to the state banquet in honor of the birth of Alexis, Yoachim objected so strenuously that the invitation was withdrawn. To make amends and perhaps also to spite the Patriarch, Peter had Gordon to dinner at Preobrazhensky the next day.

Two weeks later, the Patriarch died suddenly, but he left a legacy of his hatred for foreigners in his *Testament* to the two Tsars. It urged the immediate destruction of the Protestant churches in the German Suburb. In a thinly disguised attack on Gordon, it denounced the policy of allowing foreigners to "hold high places in the army and thus rule over Orthodox men." The warnings against the adoption of foreign customs and clothing were probably directed against Peter himself, but Peter defied them openly. Within a few days, he ordered a complete suit of German clothes and went to dine at Gordon's house in the German Suburb.

Gordon wanted greater toleration of his religion and encouraged the young Tsar to take an active part in choosing the new Patriarch. Peter favored one of the best-educated men in the Russian Church, but Natalia and the conservatives opposed him. Peter later told the Austrian ambassador that they disliked his candidate for three reasons: "1. Because he spoke barbarous languages; 2. Because his beard was not big enough for a Patriarch; and 3. Because his coachman sat upon the coach seat and not upon the horses as was usual." In the end, Peter yielded to his mother and agreed to the appointment of Adrian, a man as suspicious and reactionary as Yoachim. In his first test of strength with the conservatives Peter had lost, but he was more interested in recreation than reform.

He took increasing delight in the society of foreigners.

Gordon commanded his admiration and respect, but at fifty-five, he was three times Peter's age, and his manner was formal and stiff. A younger and far more dashing companion was one of Gordon's relations by marriage. Franz Lefort was born in Geneva and served a term as a merchant in Marseilles before becoming a soldier of fortune in Holland. Military service took him to the Baltic, and ultimately to Muscovy, where he won the favor of Vasily Golitsyn and the rank of general.

At thirty-five, Lefort was tall and well-built. He was an accomplished dancer and a fine horseman, and it was said that he could outshoot any Tartar with a bow and arrow. He was less of a scholar than Gordon, but he had picked up a fund of general information, and he spoke several languages fluently. He was witty, imaginative, and irrepressibly gay. He could adjust quickly to Peter's sudden changes of mood and match his outbursts of activity. Last but not least, he could drink "like a hero."

Drinking was Russia's national vice. The Russian Church did not discourage the use of alcohol. Drunkenness was common among its priests. It was considered a mark of respect to a saint to get drunk on his feast day. Dr. Collins, Tsar Alexis's English physician, reported that during the festival before Lent, as many as two or three hundred Russians froze to death from falling drunk into the snow.

The women drank nearly as hard as the men. As serfs drank to forget their slavery to their lords, women drank to forget their slavery to their husbands. Wife-beating was common in all classes, and it became especially vicious when the men had been drinking. Even if a wife died from a beating, her death was considered accidental. The state neither punished the husbands nor sought to curb their drunkenness. The sale of liquor was a state monopoly, and the treasury always needed money.

In his taste for drink, Peter was a true son of Russia. His capacity matched his size. Observers were astounded at the quantities of beer, wine, brandy, and vodka the giant Tsar consumed, day in and day out. It must have damaged his constitution and aggravated the convulsive spasms that began to trouble him about this time, but it did not slow the furious pace at which he lived. The aging Gordon often took to his bed for days after one of their bouts. Peter would stay up drinking all night and then spend the morning hammering at the forge or chopping trees with undiminished vigor. Both liquor and physical labor seemed to be emotional necessities for him, and both became part of his daily routine.

In the German Suburb, a typical festivity began at noon. If it involved a baptism or a wedding, Peter was often asked to act as godfather or best man. He would arrive at a gallop from Preobrazhensky with a gift he had made with his own hands—a bowl, a snuffbox, or, in later years, a model sailboat. He would perform his part in the ceremony correctly, but as soon as that was finished, he was likely to turn his back on the rest of the ritual to help himself to the caviar, herring, and vodka set out on the sideboard. He always seemed half starved. Later the whole company sat down to a banquet. They had cabbage or beet soup, suckling pig stuffed with buckwheat, roast goose, fish pies, honey cakes, salted cucumbers, pastries, and fruit, washed down with great quantities of Hungarian wine and beer. The meal was punctuated with toasts, speeches, and jokes. The amount of food and drink consumed was heroic, but the company did not linger at table all day.

Someone would suggest a game of bowls or ninepins. Others took target practice with muskets or bows and arrows. Peter enjoyed showing off in feats of strength or skill. He could straighten a horseshoe with his bare hands. Lefort made a game of throwing a handkerchief into the air so that Peter could cut it in two with his sword before it floated to the ground. They might go out for a boat race on the Yauza River, or they might have a dance.

Lefort and Peter's other foreign friends taught him to dance and, in spite of his great size, he proved a nimble and graceful dancer. All his life, he was especially fond of a country dance called *"Der Grossvater"* ("The Grandfather"). German dances required German music played on German instruments. Orthodox church music permitted only the chanting of voices and the ringing of bells. The instruments devised by the devilish cunning of the Germans made sensuous sounds calculated to seduce good Christians into sin. Patriarch Yoachim would have turned over in his grave at the spectacle of the Tsar dressed in German clothes and kicking up his heels to the unholy music of fiddles and flutes.

Dancing was one means of introducing Peter into a scandalous relationship with German women. He enjoyed their society and found their vivacity and wit a refreshing contrast to the dullness of his wife. He fell in love with Anna Mons, the daughter of a German goldsmith. She was blond, blue-eyed, and beautiful. Instead of the shapeless robes of Eudoxia, she wore a low-cut dress revealing round bare arms and shoulders, a plump bosom, and a pinched-in waist just right for squeezing. Instead of approaching him with the lowered lids and frightened mouth of Eudoxia, she looked him straight in the eye, smiling boldly, flirtatiously, even when he pulled her onto his lap. She knew how to enjoy life. All these Germans knew how to enjoy life.

There were quiet, serious moments, too. Peter came to know the pleasure of smoking a long Dutch pipe, puffing reflectively as the conversation turned on war, diplomacy, science, commerce, and manufacture. Earlier Tsars had hired foreigners to bring their technical skills to Muscovy. They had opened arms works, gunpowder factories, iron and copper mines, and mills for paper, glass, and saltpeter. If the managers of these enterprises did not actually live in the German Suburb, they kept in touch with friends who did and paid visits when they could. British and Dutch merchants who summered in Archangel had seen far more of Russia than the young Tsar. By listening to their conversation, Peter could learn a great deal about his own country.

There was also news of the outside world. Foreign diplomats, merchants, and others received letters and periodicals from many western capitals. Gordon, for example, kept up a correspondence with friends in Scotland, England, Poland, Austria, and Rome. The letters that arrived on every post day offered exciting glimpses into the great world. In the German Suburb, less than three miles from the Kremlin, Peter was learning to speak Dutch and German and forming a more vivid and comprehensive picture of the west than any Tsar before him.

Chapter **9**

THE TSAR AT PLAY

In the spring of 1690, when he was eighteen, Peter became involved in a continuous round of pleasure-seeking that lasted nearly five years. They were the years when young men today attend college, and in many ways his experience paralleled that of the present student generation. He developed a life-style radically different from that of his elders. He drew away from his mother and Muscovy as a whole. He avoided the duties and responsibilities tradition prescribed, and he became critical of traditional values. But he never seriously attacked the "establishment," partly because he *was* the establishment-and partly because he was too absorbed in the pursuit of personal pleasures.

His merrymaking was on a vast scale. He appointed Lefort his official host and added a wing to his favorite's house; but as it was common for him to dine with two or three hundred guests, even this was none too large. Later, the Tsar built a palace with a banquet hall large enough to seat fifteen hundred people, and gave it to Lefort with a generous allowance for food and drink. Lefort's parties sometimes went on for three days, and his palace became a sort of club always open to members of Peter's "company."

The "company" included from eighty to two hundred persons from very different backgrounds. Lefort was the great favorite. Other foreigners in the inner circle were Gordon, Von Mengden, Adam Weide, and Jacob Bruce. Weide and Bruce had been born in Russia, but thought of themselves as "Germans." Andrew Vinius was the son of the Dutchman. who had founded the Tula arms works at Tsar Mikhail's request. Because his mother was Russian, Andrew spoke Dutch and Russian fluently, and Peter's father had appointed him postmaster.

Peter's boyhood companions formed another part of the inner circle. Fyodor Apraxin was a kinsman to the widow of Tsar Fyodor. Andrew Matveyev was the son of the murdered minister. Aristocrats like Prince Nikita Repnin rubbed shoulders with nobodies like Alexander Menshikov, who had once sold pies in the streets of Moscow. There was a handful of men much older than Peter who managed to be friends with him across the gap of years. They included Prince Boris Golitsyn, Prince Fyodor Romodanovsky, Prince Ivan Buturlin, the two Princes Dolgoruky, and Peter's old tutor, Nikita Zotov.

All these and many more joined Peter in celebrations that became increasingly elaborate. Simply to get drunk was not enough. The party must have a central joke. Once Peter arrived at Lefort's with twenty-four dwarfs mounted on ponies. Dwarfs were a great curiosity at the time. They were kept rather like pets in most of the courts of Europe, and Peter was especially fond of them. He and Lefort rode out into the country to spend the day drilling their Lilliputian cavalry. The marriage of the court jester was the occasion of a three-day celebration in fancy costumes, climaxed by a parade into Moscow with the bridal pair mounted on a camel.

In the spring, the company celebrated the breaking up of the ice by assembling a fleet of rowboats and riding the swollen river downstream to a monastery for several days of feasting. During the Christmas holidays, Peter arranged caroling parties of eighty sledges. They were drawn by cows, goats, dogs, and pigs. The carolers were dressed in the robes of priests, bishops, and even the Patriarch.

As if this spectacle were not sacrilege enough, Peter founded an All Drunken Synod. The members dressed in costumes of the clergy and were presided over by the extutor, Zotov, as "the Prince Pope." He blessed his drunken subjects with a cross made of two pipes and sprinkled them with wine and brandy instead of holy water.

Some of Peter's amusements were dangerous. An explosion of fireworks killed three workmen and injured Timmermann. Clay pots filled with gunpowder made realistic grenades and bombs for the war games. Peter himself had his face so badly burned that he refused to attend public ceremonies for a whole summer. At another time, Gordon was wounded in the hip and confined to his bed for a week. In the fall of 1691, Prince Ivan Dolgoruky died of injuries received in a sham fight.

This was part of "a great and terrible battle" that Peter and Gordon had been planning all summer. Prince Buturlin was appointed "King of Poland," in command of several regiments of Streltsy. Prince Romodanovsky commanded the Russian army, which included the Guards, and was given the title of "Prince Caesar." Peter himself served as Captain Peter Alexeyevich. This was the beginning of a long-standing joke with undercurrents of deep seriousness. That he, the true Tsar, should serve under a Prince Caesar and work his way up through the ranks was a way of dramatizing promotion through service rather than by birth. The playboy in Peter played with fireworks, played with armies, and played with ideas as well.

In the fall of 1692, at twenty, the tremendous pace at which he had been playing finally caught up with him. He fell seriously ill. He was so near death that Prince Boris Golitsyn was said to have kept horses ready for immediate flight in case Sophia should seize power. Peter's iron constitution pulled him through, but from that time on, there was a marked increase in the convulsive spasms that disfigured his face and shook his frame in moments of fatigue or excitement. The illness taught him nothing about slowing down. At the pre-Lenten festival, he celebrated his recovery with a mammoth fireworks display, stayed up all night, and left for Peryaslavl at dawn.

He found that the lake no longer satisfied him. As he wrote later, "I then decided to see the open sea and began often to beg the permission of my mother to go to Archangel. She forbade me such a dangerous journey, but seeing my great desire and my unchangeable longing, allowed it in spite of herself." In return, Peter agreed to wait until after the celebration of his twenty-first name day and promised not to sail on open water. Apparently, he had no intention of keeping his word on this point. He wrote to Archangel to have a twelve-gun yacht prepared for his use.

To accompany him on the voyage, the Tsar took Lefort,

several other close friends, a physician, a priest, his two
favorite dwarfs, eight singers, ten Guards, and forty Streltsy. They traveled two hundred fifty miles overland to Vologda, where they boarded barges for the trip north down
the Northern Dvina River system. In the spring they would
have covered the four hundred miles on swift currents.
Now, at the height of summer, the water was shallow and
sluggish. They seemed to drift endlessly through dark forests, past mosquito-infested swamps and barren tundra,
but after two weeks, when Peter finally saw Archangel, he
knew the journey had been worth it.

There were fully a hundred ships at anchor in the river.
The smallest of them was far larger than any he had ever
seen. Their towering masts flew the flags of many nations.
Tenders plied back and forth from ship to shore. Sweating
sailors emptied and reloaded them with cargo. Bales of
hemp and sacks of grain were bound for the west in return
for casks of German or Hungarian wine. Furs of Siberian
fox, sable, and ermine were packed into holds that had
brought Dutch and English woolens. The docks were piled
high with barrels of pitch, tallow, and potash along with
bundles of uncured hides to be exchanged for firearms,
clocks, gold lace, and cloth of velvet and satin.

At Archangel Peter had his first unforgettable impression of the sea. The landlocked lake at Peryaslavl had been
broad, but this northern salt sea looked infinite. It was never
still, and its motion seemed to come from within, as if it
were breathing with a life of its own. It was mysterious, immense, untamed, and exciting.

There was another vibrant presence in the harbor. It
sang in the masts of the rigging and creaked in the oarlocks
of the tenders. It throbbed in the sea chanties of the sailors

and quickened the movements of the officers and merchants. Even old friends who had come north from the
German Suburb seemed infected by it. The intangible presence that Peter sensed in the port of Archangel was the
spirit of western commerce. It made it as different from
the German Suburb as the restless open sea is from the
placid waters of a lake.

The Tsar tried out his new yacht, the *St. Peter,* and
toured the harbor to visit foreign ships. On learning that a
great convoy of English and Dutch merchantmen would
be sailing for Europe in a few days, he arranged to accompany them in the *St. Peter* for a short distance. On August
18, they put to sea. The young Tsar was all over the ship.
He clambered into the rigging to observe the other members
of the convoy, and returned to the deck to ply the German
captain with endless questions. It was all Lefort could do
to get him below at night. They sailed for two hundred
miles before firing a farewell salute and turning back to
Archangel.

A letter from his mother awaited the young Tsar. She
complained that he had not written once since leaving
Moscow and urged his immediate return. He made light of
her charges and said that he could not leave just now, because he had to wait for the arrival of some ships from
Hamburg. This meant that he would certainly miss the
celebration of her name day on September 6, and he must
have known this would wound her deeply, but he could not
tear himself away.

Thoughts of ships and shipping possessed him. He appointed Apraxin governor of Archangel and ordered him to
build two ships for trade with the west the following summer. With his own hands, he laid the keel of a ship much

larger than the *St. Peter*. She would be called the *St. Paul*, and he intended her to explore the Siberian coast in search of a northeast passage to China. The idea had been proposed in a letter from Nicholas Witsen. Witsen was then Burgomaster of Amsterdam, but he had traded and traveled widely in Muscovy in earlier years. Peter commissioned him to purchase a 44-gun frigate in Holland.

To his mother's complaints of his absence, Peter answered that she was spoiling his fun, but, in fact, he was having the time of his life. Lefort arranged a ball or a banquet almost nightly. The next day, the Tsar sweated out the effects of the liquor in physical labor. He forged a number of iron bars and made a huge ivory chandelier from walrus tusks. With his company of singers, he joined his booming bass to the choirs of neighboring churches. He lingered long after the time he had promised his mother to depart and did not finally arrive in Moscow until October 11, more than a month after her name day.

During the fall and winter, he continued to do as he pleased. By day he turned wooden pulley blocks and cast ship's cannon for the *St. Paul*. At night he ignored his wife and son to disport himself at Lefort's palace or at the house he had given Anna Mons in the German Suburb. Over the Christmas holidays, he again organized a sledge caravan of drunken carolers, and he was in the midst of pre-Lenten festivities when word came that his mother had fallen ill in the Kremlin.

Natalia was only forty-two, and Peter did not take her condition seriously enough to pay her a visit. He was stunned five days later to hear that she was dying. Conscience-stricken, he galloped at once to the palace. Outside the sickroom, Patriarch Adrian rebuked him for coming in

German riding clothes. Peter retorted angrily that the head of the church ought to have more on his mind than tailoring, but when he saw his mother, his anger melted into remorse and grief. She lay motionless and so pale that, except for her labored breathing, she might have been already dead. Peter could not bear to watch. He fled to Preobrazhensky and sat up with Gordon through the long hours of the night. At dawn, word came that the Tsaritsa was dead.

Peter shut himself up and refused to see any but his most intimate friends. At intervals he broke into uncontrollable sobs. He could not bring himself to attend the public funeral, but afterward he made a private pilgrimage to pray beside his mother's tomb. It was a full week before he could face an evening of quiet conversation with friends at Lefort's. Then suddenly he seemed to throw off his despair. He wrote to Apraxin that, "Like Noah, resting a while from my grief and leaving aside that which can never return, I write about the living." He went on to give detailed instructions about the building of the *St. Paul*.

Instead of bringing him closer to his wife, the death of Natalia had the opposite effect. His affection for his mother had been the only influence that could overcome his revulsion for the Kremlin. His rare appearances there had been solely to please her. Now that she was gone, that tie no longer held him. After marching in the Easter procession in April, he turned his back on the Kremlin and plunged wholeheartedly into the exploration of a different world.

Chapter 10

FROM ARCHANGEL TO AZOV

In the spring of 1694, Peter and three hundred retainers set out for Archangel, where Peter was delighted to
find the *St. Paul* ready for the water. He personally knocked
away the first prop at the launching, but then came a lull.
The *St. Paul* was afloat, but she could not be sailed until
she was rigged and fitted. The Dutch frigate he had purchased had not yet arrived from Holland. Instead of waiting, he decided to make a pilgrimage to the Solovetsky
Monastery.

With the Archbishop of Kholmogory as one of his companions, he put to sea in the *St. Peter*. It was June 10, the
day after his twenty-second birthday and very nearly his
last. Eighty miles from Archangel, a violent storm carried
away all sail. The little yacht was so near swamping that the
Archbishop administered the last rites. Clinging to the
helm, Peter took Holy Communion with the others, but he
did not give up hope. With his help, the native pilot was

able to bring the ship to a safe anchorage under a lee shore. There the Tsar built with his own hands a cross nearly ten feet high and set it up to mark the spot where they had landed. In Dutch, he carved the words, "This cross was made by Captain Pieter in the summer of 1694."

Sailing on to Solovetsk, Peter spent three days in fasting and prayer. When he got back to Archangel, fasting gave way to feasting. The *St. Paul* was christened, and the arrival of the frigate from Holland required another celebration. Peter now had three Russian men-of-war ready for a sea voyage in company with a fleet of western merchant ships. Their real command was entrusted to westerners, but it was Peter's whim to appoint Romodanovsky Admiral, Buturlin Vice Admiral, and Gordon Rear Admiral. Next, he invented his own system of flag signals and had it translated into German and English, so that his flagship could send orders through the whole fleet. Sailing in the new Dutch frigate, he enjoyed the voyage even more than the one the previous summer, but the day after his return to Archangel, he hurried off to Moscow to play war on land instead of at sea.

The war games in the fall of 1694 were on the largest scale yet. A total of 15,000 men was divided into two armies. As "King of Poland," Buturlin defended a fortress the Tsar had had built on the Moscow River below the capital. As "Prince Caesar," Romodanovsky laid siege. The games continued for five weeks. Clay bombs and firepots caused a number of casualties, but it was a merry campaign. There was a troupe of dwarfs and a company of singers to provide entertainment. During frequent "truces," the popping of corks replaced the crackle of muskets, and cannon were fired only to salute the toasts. After the banquet on Lefort's name day, the "Prince Caesar's" forces were so flushed with wine that they spontaneously charged and overran the Polish fortress, but Peter would not accept this bacchanalian victory. He made the armies go through it all again in a more military manner.

The sham war was over in October. By January 1695, Peter was deep in preparations for a real one. What is more, this war was to be waged on a frontier in which Peter had previously showed no interest. After his total absorption in Archangel, he suddenly decided to attack Azov on the southern frontier. This abrupt about-face from north to south was more logical than it may seem. Moscow was close to the headwaters of rivers that flowed to four seas. The Northern Dvina River led to Archangel on the White Sea. The Don River was the road to Azov, with access to the Black Sea. Azov was held by Turks and Tartars, Muscovy's traditional enemies, and Russia had been technically at war with them ever since Sophia's disastrous Crimean campaigns of 1687 and 1689. Yet there was a new motive behind Peter's decision to reactivate the war.

Archangel had inspired Peter with dreams of a fleet and a merchant marine, but the port had two serious limitations. It was closed to navigation nine months a year, and its commerce was so dominated by skilled western merchants that the inexperienced Russians would find it difficult to compete. Peter's imagination conceived a daring alternative. In Archangel, he had seen casks of caviar destined for Italy, six thousand miles away by sea. If he could reestablish Russian power on the Black Sea, he might revive the Mediterranean commerce of Kiev Russia. A warm-water port there would give him a shorter route to the west. The conquest of Azov would be a first step in that direction. It was as simple as that.

The strategy of the campaign was more complicated. General Sheremetev would lead an army of 120,000 regulars against the Turkish fortresses on the Lower Dnieper River. The siege of Azov would be left to a smaller force of 30,000 made up of the play regiments, the foreign-trained troops, and the pick of the Streltsy. It was divided into three armies under the command of Gordon, Lefort, and Golovin. The generals were to act together, but no one had supreme command. Gordon marched 10,000 men overland. Peter and the remaining troops set out by water.

By way of the Moscow, Oka, and Volga Rivers, they made for Tsaritsyn (Stalingrad, now called Volgograd). It was a distance of more than a thousand miles, and the army of 20,000 was encumbered with artillery and supplies. The weather was bad. Snow and opposing winds caused delays.

Peter blamed most of the difficulties on the stupidity of the pilots and barge builders, but he failed to appreciate the problems of river navigation. The violence of Russia's spring floods carried down masses of ice that tore away banks and shifted channels. Trees that had toppled into the water lay lurking beneath the surface like concealed reefs. Old channels silted up, and new ones formed, so that the Volga pilots had to deal with a strange new river each spring.

Peter's impatience with the bad workmanship of the river barges was more understandable. An English merchant who had sailed on such vessels described them as "so many wrecks." Often a hundred feet long by twenty in width, they had scarcely any crossbeams for support and were fastened together with wooden pegs instead of iron bolts.

There was so little pitch and tar used that strips of bark were nailed over the seams to keep the caulking from falling out, and they leaked constantly.

The Volga of Peter's day had much in common with Mark Twain's Mississippi. Along both rivers, different races and civilizations mingled. On both, a slave-based agriculture was expanding into fertile plains and displacing primitive nomads. American Negro slaves, Indians, half-breeds, and desperadoes had their Russian counterparts in serfs, Tartar tribesmen, Cossacks, and renegades. Both countries had their runaways, their outlaws, and their rough frontier justice. When Russian patrols captured river pirates, they erected gallows on rafts. The criminals, bound hand and foot, were hung alive on iron hooks under their rib cages and set adrift to serve as an example to others.

The commerce of the Volga was growing. Barges loaded with rock salt and fish were hauled upriver from Astrakhan by sturdy boatmen. Others carried processed caviar or bales of silk that Armenian merchants had traded from Persia. As Peter's fleet continued south from Nizhni-Novgorod (today called Gorky), he saw the forests of central Russia melt into grassy steppes that stretched to a blue horizon. For miles on end, there might be no sign of human habitation, but the river was alive with fish, and great flocks of wild geese winged their way northward, honking high overhead.

At Tsaritsyn, the army disembarked and struck out overland fifty miles to the Don River. The steppes in spring were like a garden, with tulips, roses, lilies of the valley, pinks, sweet williams, and many other flowers growing in profusion. Delicious wild asparagus was plentiful, as were licorice, almond, and cherry trees. The abundant game included deer, elk, wild boar, wild horses, and wild sheep. Riding over this fertile land, Peter sensed the possibilities for development and dreamed of his country's future greatness.

On the Don, a fleet of river barges was waiting to meet the army, and the voyage continued. The Tsar finally arrived in sight of Azov on July 9. It was his twenty-third name day, and General Gordon, whose army was already encamped, invited his royal master to celebrate with dinner in his tent. From the low hill where they dined, the young Tsar could overlook the Turkish fortress. Five centuries before, it had been the site of a Genoese colony carrying on a prosperous trade with Kiev. Soon, it would be his.

Chapter 11

THE TSAR COMES OF AGE

As it approaches the sea, the Don River divides into several branches, and the fortress of Azov was built on the most southerly of these, ten miles above the mouth. A mile farther upstream, the Turks had erected fortified towers on opposite banks with a huge iron chain stretched between them to block any boats coming down the Don. All supplies for the besieging Russians had to be landed upriver and carried overland, where they were exposed to attack by marauding Tartar cavalry.

The length of the Russian supply lines was a more serious obstacle. Baggage trains often broke down on their way from the interior. For several weeks, the army was without salt, a serious lack for men digging trenches in tropical heat. By contrast, the Turks were well supplied. Shortly after Peter's arrival, twenty enemy galleys delivered fresh troops and provisions while he looked on helplessly. What good was it to construct siege works on land when the Azov garrison could be reinforced by water?

Peter had his first taste of success when his Cossacks stormed and captured the fortified towers that blocked the river, but almost at the same moment, he learned that Jacob Jansen, a Dutch officer of whom he was especially fond, had defected to the enemy. Jansen had a fund of secret information to betray to the Turkish commandant, but his most damaging revelation was a simple one. The Russians, he said, customarily took naps following their midday meal. The very next afternoon, the enemy launched a surprise attack. Twelve Russian officers and 400 men were killed. Another 600 were wounded. General Gordon narrowly escaped capture. Peter was learning the hard way that real warfare did not allow time out for rest and recreation.

The Russian generals could not agree on a plan for the siege works. The cautious and experienced Gordon wanted to run them right up to the river to cut off communication between the Azov garrison and the Tartar cavalry in the Russian rear. He also advised digging a series of trenches close to the fortress walls, so that during the final assault, the troops would be exposed to Turkish fire for only a short distance. But Peter was too impatient for such a time-consuming strategy. Lefort and Golovin sided with the Tsar, and an all-out effort to storm the walls was scheduled for August 15. It failed dismally. The Russians lost 1500 men, including several of Peter's boyhood companions from the play regiments.

One mistake followed another. An attempt to explode a pair of mines beneath the walls of Azov was so badly engineered that it left the fortress unharmed, but killed many Russians with flying debris thrown into the trenches. News that General Sheremetev had captured the Turkish fortresses on the Lower Dnieper River, three hundred miles away, encouraged Peter to insist on one more attempt to storm Azov. It failed, as might have been predicted. What was worse, it delayed the army's withdrawal into the season of rain and cold weather.

Raising the siege on October 12, the retreating Russians were slowed by mud and the raiding Tartar cavalry. In one attack nearly a whole Russian regiment was taken, but storms and floods were even more destructive than the Tartars. An Austrian envoy reported "great stores of the best provisions, which might have kept a large army for a year, either ruined by the weather or lost by the barges going to the bottom." The steppes that had seemed so friendly and fertile in the spring had been scorched by summer grass fires and soaked by fall rains. They offered neither firewood for the men nor fodder for the horses. Starvation, exposure, and disease pursued the retreating Russians. For five hundred miles, "Men and horses lay half-eaten by the wolves, and many villages were full of the sick, half of whom died."

Peter recognized that his own bad judgment had been the principal cause of the disaster, but that only steeled his determination. During the homeward march, he was already laying plans for the following spring. From Cherkassk, the capital of the Don Cossacks, he wrote orders to engage Austrian siege engineers for the next campaign. At the Tula Arms Works, where he waited for his broken army to catch up with him, he worked off his frustrations hammering out three huge metal plates at the forge. He renewed his resolve with every blow.

He saw his needs clearly. He must have a new army, and that army must have a unified command. Transport and supply would have to be improved, and he must find some way of preventing the reinforcement of Azov by the Turkish fleet. The new army would be twice the size of the old one. There would be 46,000 regulars, 20,000 Cossacks, and 3,000 Kalmyks. Peter appointed Alexis Shein as supreme commander. He would have preferred Lefort or Gordon, but Shein was a respected boyar, and the conservatives had been grumbling that Peter's defeat was due to foreign officers in high places.

The new route to Azov would bypass the Volga. The army would march to Voronezh, the nearest navigable portion of the Don River, three hundred miles south of Moscow, and go the rest of the way by water. This would require thirteen hundred river barges, and Peter planned a huge dockyard at Voronezh for the purpose. The forced labor of 30,000 serfs was needed. They had to be fed and housed, provided with timber and building materials, and taught shipbuilding. And the entire fleet must be ready in five months. It was a tremendous undertaking.

Peter saw to everything, but he was particularly concerned with the construction of thirty galleys with which he hoped to blockade the water approach to Azov. A galley he had previously ordered from Holland was already at Archangel. He had it taken apart in sections and hauled overland on sledges to Preobrazhensky to serve as a model for the others. When they were complete, they could be taken by sledge to Voronezh, reassembled, and launched in the river. In January, twenty-four foreign carpenters and the Dutch galley arrived in Preobrazhensky, and the work began.

Peter had been forced into fretful inactivity by a foot infection when he received sad news from the Kremlin. His frail half brother Ivan had suddenly died. Peter was genuinely grieved. He had been fond of Ivan, and he would demonstrate his affection by caring for his widow and daughters throughout his life; but prolonged mourning was not in his nature. Besides, he was now the sole ruler, and he had much to do. He attended Ivan's funeral, and as soon as his foot was well enough for him to travel, he set off for Voronezh.

In the wintertime, Peter generally covered more than a hundred miles in a day. Sled travel was fast and convenient. Normally, the snow was packed as hard and as smooth as ice, and the horses' rough iron shoes gave them secure footing. But during this trip, unseasonably warm weather melted the snow to a sticky mush. The three-hundred-mile journey took a full week.

The snow-covered log cabins and bustling activity of Voronezh gave it the look of an Alaskan boomtown during the gold rush, but the driving force in Voronezh was not the lure of gold, but the will of the Tsar. Peter's arrival furnished additional incentive. His gigantic figure striding through the dockyards inspired awe. This was a Tsar with the strength of three men and the energy of ten, a Tsar who could work and sweat like any peasant, a Tsar whose face could convulse and whose eyes could flash with the sudden fury of a demon. This was a Tsar who must be obeyed at all costs.

Peter was as tireless with his pen as with his ax. He dispatched a stream of demands and requests. Where were the Danish officers and shipbuilders he had sent for? When would the galleys arrive from Preobrazhensky? Voronezh lacked sufficient ash timber for galley oars. This must be cut and transported immediately from the forests around Tula.

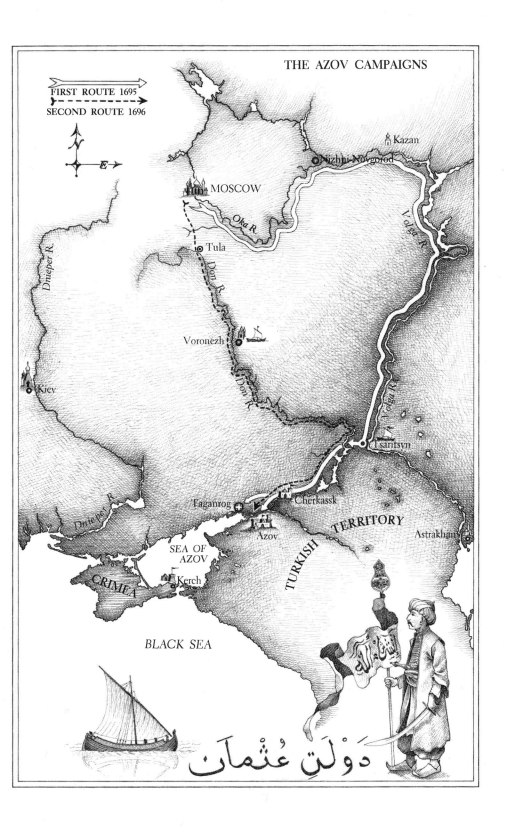

THE AZOV CAMPAIGNS

FIRST ROUTE 1695
SECOND ROUTE 1696

E

Kazan

Nizhni-Novgrod

MOSCOW

Oka R.

Volga R.

Tula

Dnieper R.

Don R.

Voronezh

Don R.

Kiev

Volga R.

Tsaritsyn

Taganrog

Cherkassk

TURKISH TERRITORY

Azov

Astrakhan

Dnieper

SEA OF
AZOV

CRIMEA

Kerch

BLACK SEA

Early in April, the spring sun turned the frozen surface of the river the color of honeycomb. The rising water beneath pressed upward until it burst the ice in a series of deafening explosions. The current ran swift, muddy, and flecked with debris washed down by the flood. Within a week, the sudden Russian spring had covered the trees with new green.

Barges and galleys were launched. Soldiers loaded cargoes of arms, ammunition, provisions, and equipment. New detachments of troops and ships headed downriver every few days. First Gordon, then Golovin, then Shein disappeared around the bend in the river. Captain Peter had to wait for the fitting of his galley, but once on his way he moved so swiftly that he overtook them at Cherkassk.

Here Peter got word that a Turkish fleet was preparing to land supplies at Azov. In command of nine galleys and forty light Cossack boats, he hurried to intercept it. At the river mouth the water was made unusually shallow by a strong wind blowing out to sea. His galleys could not cross the sand bars and had to put back, but the Cossack boats saved the day. Under cover of darkness, they captured ten supply barges and burned a larger ship to the waterline. This daring raid so unnerved the Turks that the remainder of the fleet put to sea. As soon as the wind subsided, Peter floated his galleys past the mouth of the river, where they prepared to blockade future attempts to supply Azov.

The Turks had neglected to fill in the Russian trenches of the previous summer, so that they were ready for occupancy with little digging. Peter ordered them extended to the river to cut off contact between the Turks in the fort and the Tartars on the steppe. When these Tartars attempted a surprise attack, they were repulsed so vigorously that their chieftain barely escaped with a Kalmyk arrow in his shoulder. A new Turkish fleet appeared on the horizon, but fled when Peter's galleys came out to do battle.

By June 28, the siege artillery had been mounted in place. Peter personally loaded and fired the opening gun. He was in high spirits. When his sister Natasha wrote to caution him not to go near cannonballs and bullets, he answered, "It is not I who go near cannonballs and bullets, but they who come near to me. Send orders for them to stop it."

The bombardment continued for two weeks. On July 9, 1696, Peter's twenty-fourth name day, he sent a Kalmyk bowman to arch an arrow over the walls of the town. It carried a letter that demanded surrender and offered reasonable terms. But a defiant salvo of cannon was the only Turkish answer.

The Austrian engineers had not yet arrived, so Peter's generals decided to build their siege works in the old Russian way. A force of 15,000 men set to work piling up a huge mound, which they gradually pushed forward toward the walls. By July 21, it was already high enough to fire down into the town. The Austrian engineers arrived too late to suggest improvements on the mound, but their direction of the siege artillery helped to open a small breach in the walls.

The campaign came to an unexpected climax soon afterward. The Cossacks were exasperated by the heavy labor of earthmoving and took matters into their own hands. Acting without orders, 2,000 of them climbed the mound and charged into the town. Golovin sent regular troops to the Cossack support. Before Shein could order a general assault, the Turks began waving their turbans in surrender. Their supplies of ammunition were nearly exhausted.

Peter allowed the Turkish troops, with their wives and

children, to depart in peace, but he insisted on having the Dutch traitor, Jacob Jansen, delivered to him. Jansen was carried into the Russian camp bound hand and foot, pleading for the mercy of a quick death. Peter later had him brought to Moscow, where he was paraded through the streets, knouted, tortured, and finally beheaded.

At Azov, following the victory banquet, Peter ordered the trenches filled and the mound leveled. He asked the Austrian engineers to design improved fortifications. The reconstruction of Azov was begun in a few days. He himself sailed off in his galley to seek a harbor deep enough for seagoing vessels beyond the shallow mouth of the Don River. Finding a suitable anchorage at a place called Taganrog, he returned to Azov and began his journey north. On October 10, he entered Moscow in triumph.

Muscovy had not won a military victory since early in the reign of Peter's father, and enthusiasm ran high, but people were puzzled by the Tsar's way of celebrating. There were no priests or bishops in the procession. Instead of attending mass and receiving the blessing of the Patriarch, the army simply marched under a triumphal arch in the manner of pagan Rome, a thing unheard of in Holy Russia. The Tsar was dressed in a plain dark blue uniform of German cut with a white feather in his cap, and he marched on foot, like a common soldier, while the "German" Lefort rode ahead in a gold coach.

The novel procession celebrated a new kind of warfare. Azov had fallen less to military heroics than to the careful organization and planning of the Russian campaign. The genius of that organization was the young giant with the white feather in his cap. Tsar Peter had come of age.

Chapter 12

THE GREAT EMBASSY

For the spectators of Peter's triumphant entry into Moscow, the capture of Azov seemed an end in itself. For Peter, it was only a beginning. He had won his way into the Sea of Azov, but the Turkish fortress of Kerch still commanded the straits that opened into the Black Sea. His ambition resembled the lower reaches of the Don River: its mainstream divided into separate channels, but all its mouths emptied into the same sea. Now all Peter's separate programs aimed toward the same goal: the creation of a Russian fleet on the Black Sea.

He had begun planning construction of this fleet even before the Turkish surrender. In July, he had written to Venice to ask for "thirteen worthy shipwrights able to build every kind of seagoing vessel." Back in the capital, his programs developed rapidly. One decree commanded 3,000 peasant families from Kazan and 3,000 Streltsy from Moscow to resettle in Azov. Another drafted 20,000 peasants from the Ukraine to build the harbor at Taganrog.

Peter forced through the Council of Boyars a plan for constructing large ships. The main cost was charged to the landlords, and the estates of the church were taxed one quarter higher than those of the nobles. Every church or monastery with 8,000 peasant households, and every noble with 10,000, had to provide one ship. Lesser landowners were formed into companies, and each company was responsible for one ship on the same basis as the great landowners. The government furnished ship timber, but rigging, fitting, armament, and everything else had to be provided by the landowners. Ships were to be constructed at Voronezh. They must be ready for launching by April, 1698. The merchants of Muscovy were first assigned twelve ships, but when they dared to protest, Peter raised their quota to fourteen.

The building that was so costly to the Russians was very profitable to "Germans." Natives knew nothing about shipbuilding and had to hire foreign contractors to supervise the work. Franz Timmermann was one of a number of westerners who did a thriving business. Foreign shipwrights were also in great demand. By January, at least fifty builders had arrived from Venice, Holland, England, Denmark, and Sweden.

Peter was forced to depend on foreigners for the moment, but he planned to train Russians to build and sail his ships in the future. He ordered sixty-one sons of great boyars to Italy, Holland, and England to study the art of shipbuilding and navigation. They would live and travel at their own expense, and would not be permitted to return without a certificate of proficiency in their studies. Their families were horrified.

Land travel was slow, difficult, dangerous, and expensive. Sea voyages were cheaper and faster, but Archangel, Russia's only port, was more than six hundred miles from Moscow and open to navigation only three months a year. From there it took at least six weeks to sail to London or Amsterdam and four or five months to reach Italy by sea.

Physically, Moscow was closer to western Europe than were the American colonies, but psychologically, it was much farther away. Most Americans were only a generation removed from western Europe. They shared common languages, traditions, and institutions. Muscovites did not even have the same alphabet. The language barrier was a tremendous obstacle. In commanding his subjects to study in the west, Peter was sentencing them to a prolonged exile from their families, friends, and even their religion.

To cap the climax, the Tsar announced that he, too, would travel abroad. For the past six centuries, no Russian ruler had ever left his country except to make war, but Peter was deaf to conservative protests. He was not going to leave the shipbuilding to his people. "A monarch would feel ashamed to lag behind his subjects in any craft."

The trip would take the form of a "Great Embassy." All the tasks assigned to this embassy were aimed at putting a Russian fleet on the Black Sea. The embassy would seek allies for a new campaign against the Turks. It would recruit sea captains, gunnery experts, and specialists in the shipbuilding art. It would purchase naval supplies and arms. Finally, it would offer the Tsar the protective camouflage to preserve his privacy while he studied shipbuilding. He would travel incognito as Bombardier Peter Mikhailov, while his ambassadors would take the limelight.

As ambassadors, Peter appointed Franz Lefort, Fyodor Golovin, the kinsman of the general, and Prokofy Voznitsyn, a veteran diplomat. There were forty "volunteers" to study shipbuilding. With priests, interpreters, dwarfs, singers, and servants, the embassy included 250 persons in all.

Peter's preparations included arrangements to govern the country in his absence, and here too he was especially concerned with any program that would contribute to the goal of a Black Sea fleet. As if the constructions at Voronezh, Taganrog, and Azov were not sufficiently ambitious, he approved a proposal to link the Don and Volga rivers by way of a gigantic canal, requiring more thousands of forced laborers. When finished, it would give him an all-water route from Moscow to the Sea of Azov.

The Tsar was almost ready for his departure, and was enjoying a banquet at Lefort's palace, when two figures from the past cast ominous shadows across his path. A certain Yelissov accused a small group headed by Colonel Tsykler with conspiracy and treason. There was no real conspiracy, and the so-called treason was probably nothing more than grumbling at the expense of the shipbuilding program at Voronezh, but Yelissov was one of the Streltsy spies who years before sent word to Preobrazhensky that Sophia had ordered an attack, and Tsykler was a Streltsy officer who had come to the Troitsa Monastery to make accusations against her. It gave Peter a terrifying sense of reliving the nightmare memories of his youth, and he lost his head. Tsykler and his companions were put to torture, and one by one, they "confessed" to being part of a Miloslavsky conspiracy. Tsykler and four others were sentenced to death.

The macabre revenge Peter concocted for the dead Ivan Miloslavsky suggests that he was temporarily deranged. It resembled a savage ritual of black magic to lay a ghost. Miloslavsky's coffin was unearthed from its grave, dragged through the streets by swine, and placed beneath the execution platform. After removing the lid, the executioner cut off the arms, legs, and heads of the condemned traitors, so that their blood splattered on what was left of Ivan Miloslavsky.

A stone column was erected in the Red Square. The butchered remains of the conspirators were hung from it with a description of their crimes written on a sheet of tin. For five months, under spring rains and summer sun, they served as grisly reminders of Peter's grim determination and demoniac rage. With this act of Asiatic cruelty behind him, the young Tsar prepared to expose himself to the civilization of Europe.

Chapter **13**

THREE WESTERN NEIGHBORS

On the morning of March 19, 1697, five days after the executions, the Great Embassy left Moscow. Whips cracked. Sleigh bells jingled. The slanting sunlight glowed in the vaporing breaths of bearded coachmen and shaggy horses. Roughshod hoofs scattered glittering ice chips as the caravan of sledges streamed across the snowy landscape. Behind them the bronze onion domes, gilded cupolas, and blood-red battlements of the Kremlin gave it the look of a Muscovite Camelot, but Peter was too intent on the journey to look backward. His mind's eye focused on the harbors, ships, and dockyards of Holland. It would be five long months before he beheld them in person. The first foreign soil Peter touched belonged to Sweden.

During the Thirty Years War, the Swedes had conquered so much of the coast of the Baltic Sea that it had become a sort of Swedish lake. Its most valuable port was Riga, which the Great Embassy entered early in April. Governor General Dahlberg knew of the Tsar's presence, and it put him in a delicate position. He had to play host to one of his country's traditional enemies. In fact, Peter's father had tried to storm Riga only forty years before. Moreover, Dahlberg was not expecting so large a retinue, and he had to provide for 250 Russians during a serious local famine. The ice on the Düna River had broken up. The ice floes made it dangerous to attempt to cross in boats, and the floating bridge used during the summer could not be put in place until the floodwaters had subsided. Therefore, the Embassy's departure might be postponed indefinitely.

Peter soon became restless. During the shipping season, Riga was a far busier port than Archangel. It had a virtual monopoly of the largest masts of Europe. They were floated downstream from the forests of Poland in great rafts of five hundred to a thousand logs each. But at the moment, both the port and the river were idle. Walking around the city, Peter was irritated to find that his great size and exaggerated gestures made him the center of curious crowds wherever he went.

Then came the crowning insult. On a tour of the fortifications, he was taking the measurements of a moat when a sentry ordered him away at gunpoint. He was wearing the uniform of a bombardier, and he had no business measuring an enemy fortress on the frontier, but he was outraged. Leaving the main body of the Embassy behind, he took Lefort and a few companions, crossed the river in spite of the drifting ice, and hurried on.

Peter was now entering the territory of the Holy Roman Empire, but at this period, as Voltaire was to quip, it was neither holy, Roman, nor an empire. It was not holy, because the wars of the Reformation had shattered its religious unity. It was not Roman, because the vast majority of its people were Germanic. It was not an empire, but a loose federation of three thousand semi-independent feudal states, ranging from large principalities like Saxony and Hanover down to the tiny territories of free knights. The title of Emperor was not hereditary, but elective. He was chosen by nine hereditary Electors. For nearly two centuries, it had been the practice to elect the heir to the Austrian House of Hapsburg, but at each election, the Hapsburg heir had to bargain away so much in return for their votes that the Emperor's control over the German Electors was growing steadily weaker.

Frederick von Hohenzollern of Brandenburg was one of these Electors. He was actively working to transform his territory into the independent Kingdom of Prussia. As soon as he learned that the conqueror of Azov had arrived in his port city of Pilau, he invited Peter to dine.

The two men were a study in contrasts. Frederick was forty, clean-shaven, and elegantly dressed. Peter was twenty-five, with a dark wisp of a moustache, and pipe ash spilled on his shabby vest. Frederick was a man of the world. Peter resembled a peasant whose great horny hands threatened to upset the delicate porcelain and glassware on the dinner table. Frederick was a veteran of European diplomacy. Peter was a novice and he listened warily to the proposals that the older man wove into his conversation.

Their immediate interests did not coincide. Frederick wanted independence from the Austrian Emperor and an alliance against Sweden, but no part of a war with Turkey. Austria was Peter's ally against the Sultan, and he wanted allies to fight Turkey, not Sweden. He did not commit himself, but he took note of Frederick's suggestion that a fleet on the Baltic might offer greater advantages than one on the Black Sea.

Despite the differences in age, education, and objectives, the two men liked each other, and Frederick went out of his way to make Peter's visit enjoyable. He arranged for the Tsar to watch a bear-fight, inspect an arsenal, and spend a full week taking gunnery instruction in the Royal Artillery Park. Peter was impressed by the efficiency and orderliness of the country. Prussian gunpowder burned with a fine white smoke and, unlike the Russian, seldom misfired. The streets were paved with cobblestones instead of timber. There was an amazing variety of goods in the shops, and in the houses people left valuable objects on tabletops or open shelves, as if thieving were unknown in this country.

Meeting Frederick on board his yacht, Peter agreed verbally, but not in writing, to assist him against their mutual enemies. These vague assurances concluded his diplomatic business with his host, but Peter remained as his guest for another month to follow political developments inside Poland.

The Polish monarchy was elective, and because the unruly and self-seeking nobles often sold their votes to the highest bidder, the election of a new king was an invitation to foreign intervention. In the election of 1697, there were two principal contenders. If the French candidate won, Poland would certainly make peace with Turkey, France's traditional ally. For this reason, Peter preferred another foreigner, Augustus of Saxony. He posted several regiments of Streltsy on Poland's eastern frontier, and just before the election, he sent to Warsaw a strong statement of support for Augustus. The moment he heard the news that Augustus was elected the new Polish king, the Tsar left for Holland. He could now turn his full attention to the study of shipbuilding.

Chapter 14

WHAT THE TSAR LEARNED IN HOLLAND

On August 6, 1697, the Great Embassy rolled into the little town of Koppenbrügge, close to the Dutch frontier. As his carriage jolted past the rustic castle, Peter noticed a crowd collecting by the gate. Later, as he sat over beer with Franz Lefort at the local inn, he discovered what it meant. An elegant courtier appeared and, in the most flowery German, begged His Tsarish Majesty to be so good as to accept an invitation to dine with his mistress, Princess Sophia, the Electress of Hanover.

Sophia was the mother-in-law of Frederick, Peter's host in Prussia. Her daughter, Sophia Charlotte, had been on an extended visit in Hanover when Peter had arrived in Pilau. Letters from Frederick about the strange visitor from Muscovy had whetted the curiosity of both mother and daughter. When they learned that he would pass through the nearby village of Koppenbrügge, they set out especially to intercept him.

If Peter had followed his first impulse, their journey

would have been for nothing. His dread of being stared at was growing. Only days before, rowdy university students had forced their way into his lodgings to get a glimpse of him. He wanted to refuse Sophia's invitation outright, but Lefort pointed out that this would be considered a sign of Muscovite backwardness. Peter relented on certain conditions. He must be let in privately by a back way. He would dine only with the members of Sophia's immediate family. Lefort and his nephew would accompany him as interpreters. The other members of the embassy must be entertained in another part of the castle.

Sophia Charlotte described the moment of their meeting in a letter. When the towering Tsar had entered by a back way from the garden, he stood uncertainly as mother and daughter greeted him. For a moment he hesitated, reddened, then suddenly hid his face in his hands.

"*Ich kann nicht sprechen,*" he said. They were the only German words he could remember at the moment. "I can't talk."

Lefort stepped forward to cover his master's embarrassment, expressed the Tsar's great pleasure at their meeting, and guided Peter through the introductions. When they sat down to dine, Lefort translated the questions with which the two ladies peppered the Tsar, but after a glass or two of wine, Peter's German came back to him, and he began to speak for himself.

Soon, they were all talking and laughing with animation. Peter and Sophia Charlotte exchanged snuffboxes. His was one he had made himself on the turning lathe. He showed the ladies the calluses on his hands and told them that he was master of seventeen trades. In the end, he became so merry that he asked that the other party be

N

NORTH SEA

SWEDEN

FINLAND

L.

KARI

Future Site of
ST. PETERSBURG

ING

ESTONIA

STOCKHOLM

BALTIC SEA

LIVONIA

Riga

Mitau

COURLAND

Düna

ENGLAND

AMSTERDAM

Copenhagen

Pilau

Königsberg

LONDON

HOLLAND

HANOVER

Rhine R.

BRANDENBURG

POLAND

ENGLISH CHANNEL

Dresden
SAXONY

C

Rava

P

PARIS

AUSTRIA

VIENNA

MOL

Danube R.

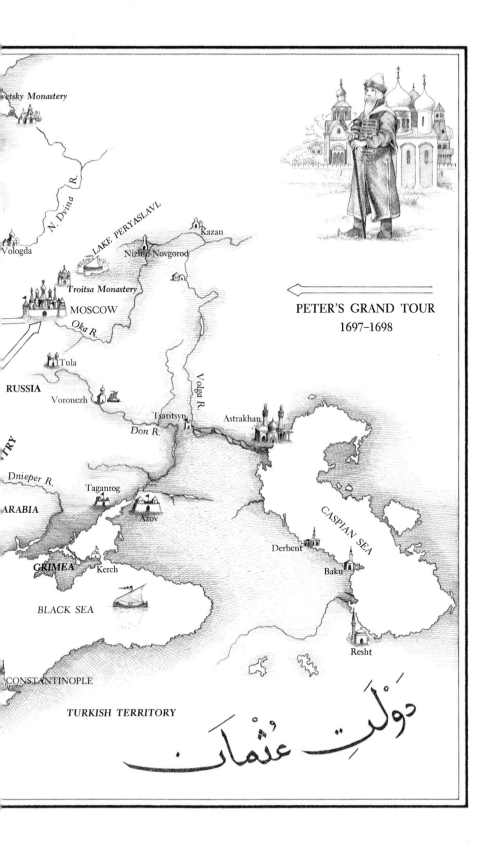

joined to theirs and ordered his musicians to play, so that they might all dance.

Both mother and daughter formed a high opinion of Peter. They noticed his awkward table manners and poor German, but were not disconcerted by the involuntary nervous spasms that occasionally contorted his handsome face, and they admired his intelligence, curiosity, and liveliness. Although they were at table for four hours, Sophia regretted that it was not longer, "for his society gave us much pleasure. He is a very extraordinary man. It is impossible to describe him or even to give an idea of him, unless you have seen him. He has a very good heart and remarkably noble sentiments. I must tell you also that he did not get drunk in our presence."

The next morning, Peter resumed his journey. With a few companions, he left the main body of the embassy to sail down the Rhine River. Natives of Zaandam he had known in Russia had convinced him that it was the shipbuilding capital of the world. He was so eager to reach it that he sailed past Amsterdam without stopping. As his ship moved up the Zaan River, he scanned the shore curiously.

Holland was as flat as any steppe, but it gave no sense of the vastness of the Russian landscape. The steppe was wild, deserted, boundless; Holland was like a carefully tended garden, densely peopled, divided and subdivided by dikes, canals, and fences. There were lines and boundaries everywhere. The farms stood side by side, squeezing out the wilderness between them into neat hedgerows that separated one field from another. The water was trained into canals. The very air had been tamed to turn windmills that ground wheat into flour and sawed logs into planks. All nature was domesticated to serve man.

Ahead on the river, a stout Dutchman sat in a rowboat with a fishing pole. Suddenly, a wriggling eel broke the surface of the water. He jerked it into his boat, seized it deftly, and gave it three smart blows on the head with a boathook. Peter gave a start of recognition.

"Well done, Mynheer Gerrit!" he called out. "You never struck better on the anvil."

Gerrit Kist was a native Zaandamer whom Peter had known as a blacksmith in Archangel. Peter was delighted to see a familiar face and was even more pleased by Kist's invitation to stay in his house. It had only two small rooms and a sort of sleeping closet, but this was just what Peter preferred. In Russia, rooms were kept small and low to make them easy to heat, and despite his great height, Peter was always happier in a small room. The spaciousness of western palaces made him uneasy, and Kist's tiny cottage struck him as cozy.

Early the next morning, the Tsar bought a set of carpenter's tools and went down to enroll in one of the shipyards, but he found that Zaandam had its drawbacks. A Zaandamer in Muscovy had written news of Peter's forthcoming visit, and everyone knew that the Tsar was in their midst. Some curious episodes followed.

Peter bought a hatful of plums and was strolling along eating them, when he met a crowd of boys. He gave plums to some, but there were not enough to go around, and when he laughed at those who got none, they began to throw mud and stones at him. The hero of Azov fled and took refuge in an inn, where he sent for the Burgomaster. The good man immediately issued a proclamation forbidding "insults to personages who wish to be unknown."

Peter purchased a yacht, but when he sailed it on the Zaan, so many spectators gathered on the bank that he lost his temper. Leaping ashore, he gave one of them a clout on the ear. The others burst into laughter and told the victim that he should feel honored that the Tsar of Muscovy had dubbed him a knight. Once again, Peter hid himself in an inn and refused to leave until dark.

The Burgomaster made special arrangements for a private viewing of the transfer of a large ship from one arm of the river to another across a dike by means of rollers, pulleys, and winches. It was just the sort of mechanical feat Peter enjoyed, but the mobs who flocked around knocked down the private enclosure reserved for him, and he refused to attend. Instead, he boarded his yacht and sailed off to Amsterdam.

Here, at last, he met Burgomaster Witsen, who had been his purchasing agent for the Dutch frigate and the galley that had served as the model for the Azov fleet. Witsen showed him his private museum of ship models and a splendid marine library. He arranged a sham naval fight between real warships and topped it off with a huge banquet and fireworks display. But to Peter all this was nothing compared to what he told him that night.

Witsen explained that he was a director of the East India Company and that the other directors had agreed to accept Peter as a workman on the wharf. He could live incognito in the house of a ropemaker in the privacy of the company compound. Finally, they had agreed to build a new frigate, so that Peter could follow the progress of a single ship from start to finish. The Tsar could scarcely contain himself. As soon as the light of the last fireworks had died, he sailed three hours back to Zaandam, picked up his tools, and sailed back again. Without having gone to bed, he reported for work at the East India Wharf that same morning.

Peter had come to Europe to learn, and the next few months were a period of intensive schooling. At the simplest level, he studied shipbuilding. He and ten companions worked under the master shipwright, Gerrit Claes Pool. Peter enjoyed the physical labor and the experience of being treated as a workman. When an English visitor asked Pool to indicate the Tsar of Muscovy, Pool answered by shouting, "Hey, Carpenter Pieter, why don't you give your comrades a hand?" Without a word, a dark-haired young giant laid down his saw and hurried to put his shoulder beneath a huge timber the others had been trying to lift.

At first, Peter was enthusiastic about Dutch shipbuilding. He wrote home full of excitement after the laying of the keel in September. But he did not even bother to mention the launching two months later. He had lost faith in the Dutch. Pool had no answers for many of his questions. From Russia he had written Witsen to send him the specifications of various types of ships, but the Burgomaster had put him off, and now he knew why. The Dutch had no such specifications and no scientific principles of design. Each shipwright built differently, proportioning his ships to suit his personal preference.

But if Dutch shipbuilding was disappointing, Dutch science and technology were not. Peter managed to see and do an amazing amount in a short time. He made paper in Zaandam, inspected the botanical gardens at Leyden, and learned the use of the microscope at Delft. He attended surgical lectures and dissections and in after years put what he had learned to use by performing many operations. He took lessons from a traveling dentist and later accumulated a whole bag full of teeth wrenched from the jaws of luck-less friends or retainers suffering from toothaches. He cobbled himself a pair of shoes. He studied etching and drew an allegorical picture of Christianity victorious over Islam.

In the process, Peter was discovering something far more important than any particular skill or branch of science. He was absorbing that breathtaking notion of the Renais-sance: that man could fashion his own destiny by reason and will. Human reason and human will. He was anticipat-ing the eighteenth century's faith in the idea of progress.

Muscovy had had no part in the Renaissance, and the typical Muscovite was much closer to the Middle Ages than the eighteenth century. Faith counted more than reason. Tradition was sacred. Change was heresy. Old Believers chose death by fire to changing the way they made the sign of the cross. The governor of Astrakhan opposed the canal to link the Don and the Volga rivers, because "God had made the rivers to flow one way, and it was presump-tion in man to think to turn them another." The Dutch had wrested the very land they lived on from the sea. If that was presumption, Peter was all for it.

Most members of the Great Embassy were less conserva-tive than the average Russian, but the strangeness of Hol-land was a trial. Home and Moscow were not only hundreds of miles, but hundreds of years behind them. The trip to Amsterdam was like a voyage into a distant century, and they sometimes suffered from future shock. In a surgical dissecting room, Peter's companions shrank from the corpses. The Tsar flew into a rage and forced them to tear at the exposed muscles with their teeth. It was a cruel punishment, but he would have argued that there could be no progress for people too timid to face facts of science, and he was teaching them to accept progress.

One thing Peter did not learn in Holland or anywhere else was tolerance of opposition. His savage temper and absolute power made it easy for him to overreact. On one occasion while in Amsterdam, he suddenly had two of his nobles clapped in irons. The records do not make clear what their offense had been, but Peter wanted them put to death. Witsen argued that this could not be legally done without a trial in the Dutch courts. The affair was settled by a compromise and the Russians were exiled to Dutch island colonies in distant parts of the globe.

From time to time Peter laid aside his carpenter's tools to try diplomacy. In September he went to Utrecht for an interview with William of Orange. William was both Stadholder, or chief executive, of Holland, and King of England, and Peter admired him as the architect of an alliance that had united most of the great powers in a war against Louis XIV of France. Technically they were still at war, but peace negotiations were under way in William's palace at Ryswick. Thus, Holland was a center of diplomatic activity at the time of Muscovy's debut on the European stage.

Peter twice attended formal diplomatic ceremonies with his Great Embassy. Much as he disliked protocol, he grasped the importance of making a good first impression.

The receptions and banquets went off well. The Russian ambassadors called on and received the embassies of all the great powers except France.

The family of nations that Peter was seeking to join was a queer one. The separate states of Europe shared a common religious and cultural ancestry. There were striking family resemblances in their arts and crafts, manners and customs, social systems and institutions. Yet each member state considered itself absolutely independent of the others, and each was engaged in a fierce and continuous competition with the rest.

The main rule governing their rivalry was the principle of the balance of power. No one nation could be allowed to become so strong that it could dominate all the others. When France under Louis XIV threatened to become supreme, England, Holland, Spain, Austria, Sweden, and Saxony all combined against her. But alliances of this sort were not very stable, because each state was seeking not simply a balance of power, but a favorable balance of power. Since what was favorable to one state was unfavorable to another, the search for a balance led frequently to war, and warfare was a principal function of the state.

The mercantile competition was as fierce as the military. The goal was a favorable balance of trade. Each state tried to increase its own exports, while restricting those of its rivals. Mother countries forbade others to trade with their colonies, but carried on a smuggling trade with the colonies of others. Monopolies, restrictions, fair means and foul were all part of the mercantile power struggle.

At the time of the Great Embassy the situation in the west was unfavorable to Peter's plans. He hoped that peace with France would free England, Holland, and Austria for war against Turkey. He did not realize that even as they were negotiating for peace, they were already preparing for renewed warfare. This time the prize would be the throne of Spain. The ailing Spanish King had no direct heirs, and his death would open the way to rival claims by the Austrian and French royal families. If an Austrian ascended the throne of Spain, Austria's English and Dutch allies might hope for a profitable share of the trade with Spain's colonies. If a French claimant won, that trade would go to France. For this reason, Holland and England had no thought of fighting Turkey, and the Emperor of Austria wanted peace with the Sultan to free his armies for another assault on Louis XIV. The young Tsar had come all the way from Moscow, only to have his plans wrecked by the impending battle for a throne at the other end of Europe. As an introduction into diplomatic society, his Great Embassy was a notable success. As an effort to enlist active aid against Turkey, it was a dismal failure.

Chapter 15

THE TSAR IN ENGLAND

As Peter was finishing work on the Dutch frigate in Amsterdam, he received a letter from an English Admiral, Lord Carmarthen. It begged to inform His Tsarish Majesty that King William wished to give him his new yacht, the *Royal Transport*. Carmarthen had designed her himself, and he could promise that she was trim, swift, and well-fitted. To Peter, the generosity of the English King was in shining contrast to the stinginess of the Dutch States-General. Peter had been asking for grants of money and naval supplies for his campaign against Turkey, and though it was obvious that the Dutch had more than enough of both, the miserly fellows kept putting him off. Now here was William volunteering his own yacht without even being asked.

Peter was all eagerness to go to England. He wanted to see and sail the new yacht. William's friendliness in offering it also encouraged him to hope that an alliance with England was still possible. Finally, he wanted to study English shipbuilding. He had met an Englishman who assured him that English builders, unlike Dutch, had developed scientific principles. Since Carmarthen had designed the *Royal Transport*, Peter felt he might be the very man to teach him.

Arrangements were made, and on January 18, 1698, Peter, Menshikov, and fifteen companions left the main body of the Great Embassy in Holland and rowed out to where a British squadron of two warships, two yachts, and a sloop lay at anchor. The flagship *York* was a 74-gun ship of the line, a type that was to be the backbone of the British navy for more than a century to come. She seemed huge to Peter. She had four times the bulk of the Dutch frigate he had been building. Her massive yellow-painted walls were broken by two rows of red gunports. The black muzzles that gaped through them must be capable of tremendous broadsides. Above the hull towered three tiers of masts and spars braced with a bewildering variety of stays, halyards, and lines. As he took them all in, Peter's dark eyes danced with pleasure.

On deck, he was further pleased to discover that Admiral Mitchell spoke Dutch, the foreign language he understood best. Since they would not sail until morning, Mitchell proposed a tour of the ship, and they went over her from top to bottom. Both during the inspection and after, Peter plied his host with questions, and the two men talked far into the night.

The next morning, the wind had risen sharply. Whitecaps flecked the wintry gray waters of the North Sea. The waves sent showers of spray over the chanting sailors who circled the windlass to haul in the dripping anchor cable. Aloft, the topmen clung to the yards like great birds roosting in the trees of the masts. The ship's master bawled through his speaking trumpet. Above the bowsprit, a jib bloomed and took the wind with a sound of distant thunder. One sail after another flowered, boomed, and stiffened. Each time the ship stretched another of its white canvas wings, the masts and shrouds groaned and the stays shivered. The whole hull trembled for a moment before easing forward with a sure increase of speed.

The wind blew a gale during the entire crossing. The following morning, they were in sight of the coast of Suffolk. A mile from the mouth of the Thames, Mitchell and his Russian guests had to leave the deep-drafted *York* for the yacht *Mary*. Sailing up one of the busiest waterways in the world, the *Mary* dropped anchor beside the Tower of London the following morning, January 21, 1698.

London thoroughly dominated the life of England. It was the King's residence as well as the seat of government. It was the commercial, financial, and cultural capital of the country and its busiest port. Although the Great Fire had destroyed more than half the inner city in 1666, a new and more beautiful metropolis had risen from the ashes. The architectural genius of Sir Christopher Wren contributed 53 churches and the Cathedral of St. Paul to the reconstruction. The city was throbbing with vitality.

Mitchell escorted the Tsar to a modest house on the waterfront. The winter was so severe that the Thames was frozen solid above London, where the *Royal Transport* was moored. Peter was disappointed not to take possession of her immediately, but he found much to interest him in London, and with Mitchell as his guide and interpreter, he stayed for a month.

Soon after his arrival, he had a private visit from King William. The Tsar received the King in his shirt sleeves in the small room where he and three companions had been living and sleeping for three days without once opening a window. The air was so stale and heavy with tobacco that William, who suffered from asthma, stayed only a half hour. When the Tsar paid a return call, the King persuaded him to sit for a portrait by Sir Godfrey Kneller. *cop. 2*

Peter inspected many factories and workshops. He was so intrigued by a visit to the watchmaker John Cart that he learned to take apart and reassemble the movements of a watch. Everywhere he collected plans, specifications, or models to send back to Russia. His eye was always alert for what could be useful at home. Aware that the Russian practice of hollowing out coffins from a single block of oak was far more wasteful of this essential shipbuilding timber than the English method of building with planks, he bought an English coffin.

In February, Peter and his companions moved a few miles downriver to Deptford. They were quartered in Sayes Court, the country house of John Evelyn. It was elegantly furnished and famous for its landscaped gardens, but for Peter its chief virtue was its location next door to the Royal Dockyards. Evelyn's servant reported that the new tenant was "very seldom at home a whole day, very often in the King's Yard or by the water," and one of the shipwrights remarked, "The Tsar of Muscovy works with his own hands as hard as any man in the yard."

He went to bed early and rose at four o'clock, a habit "which very much astonished those Englishmen who kept company with him." One of these was Lord Carmarthen, whose love of ships, drinking, and practical jokes made him a perfect match for Peter. A less likely caller was the scholarly Bishop Burnet, but he was impressed by Peter's reasoning in theological discussion and concluded, "He will either perish in the way or become a great man."

Burnet had noticed the Tsar's weakness for brandy, and the drunken brawls of the Russian tenants left Sayes Court a shambles. Afterward, a committee headed by Sir Christopher Wren assessed the damages, and its report ran several pages. There were three hundred broken windowpanes, twenty pictures with torn canvases and damaged frames, and more than fifty broken chairs. The floors were covered with ink and grease. Curtains and bedclothes were ripped and torn. Reparations were set at £300.

Here was another example of Peter's contradictory nature. He took care to conserve the oak of Russian coffins, but thoughtlessly destroyed the cherry and walnut of English chairs. He could be cultivated in conversation with strangers and barbarous in recreation with his companions. He had the patience and dexterity to assemble a watch as well as the recklessness and abandon to ruin a house.

The vandalism may be partially explained by ignorance. Peter was unaccustomed to such elegant furnishings and without Lefort to instruct him, may not have realized their value. Moreover, he was under great emotional strain. All day, his reason struggled to understand abstract principles of naval design and the strangeness of an unfamiliar culture. At night, it was a relief to get drunk in the good old Russian way. Finally, there must have been an element of envy tinged with malice. Everything he saw around him, the most commonplace articles and artifacts, proclaimed the technical and artistic superiority of England. Leaded glass windows and realistic oil paintings made the mica panes and crude ikons of home seem ridiculous. A drunken brawl in which he and his companions smashed these taunting reminders of British superiority was a way of soothing wounded national pride.

If King William had any inkling of the havoc at Sayes Court, he made no sign. The overriding goal of his foreign policy was to curb the power of Louis XIV, and Peter was useful to that end. He had captured the fortress of one of France's allies at Azov and blocked Louis' attempt to put a kinsman on the throne of Poland. William was unwilling to offer Peter direct military assistance against Turkey, but he was eager to court his good will and continued to show him every courtesy.

In March, Mitchell took Peter down to Portsmouth to witness a sham naval battle. An entire fleet was formed into two lines, and the battle was staged with such authentic detail that sand was sprinkled on the decks to avoid slipping on the imaginary blood. The thundering broadsides and the precision with which the ships maneuvered to close and fire again had Peter in transports. For years afterward, he used to say that it was a better life to be an admiral in England than a Tsar in Russia.

The infant Greenwich Observatory was only a short distance from Deptford. Confidently, it had declared itself to be at zero degrees longitude, the starting point for measuring the circumference of the earth. This confidence was ultimately justified. The fleets of the world would one day navigate with charts drawn to Greenwich specifications and chronometers set to Greenwich Mean Time. Peter was fascinated by navigational problems and had several long conversations with Flamsteed, the Royal Astronomer.

Peter paid repeated visits to the Tower of London. It housed the Mint, as well as a museum, an arsenal, and a prison. His principal interest in the Tower was the Mint.

Its Warden at the time was England's great physicist, Sir Isaac Newton, and the forthcoming visit of the Tsar is noted in Newton's diary, but there is no record of their meeting. In any case, Peter was less interested in the laws of motion than in the machinery of coinage.

England's coinage had recently been reformed to combat the practice of "clipping," a popular form of petty thievery. Shaving or clipping off bits of gold or silver from coin had become so widespread that many coins in circulation had lost almost half their weight and value. Clipping was difficult to detect on coins with smooth round edges, like those on our nickels or pennies. The introduction of milled edges, like those on our dimes and quarters, made it obvious. This innovation had given England the finest coinage in Europe. Realizing that Russia had the worst, Peter studied the operation of the Mint carefully.

He paid brief visits to Oxford, Windsor Castle, and the Houses of Parliament, attended a Quaker meeting, and discussed it afterward with William Penn, but random sightseeing was not to his taste. As the time for departure approached, he concentrated on recruiting British technical experts into his service. The King had granted him permission to recruit, and Carmarthen offered helpful advice. Among others, he recommended a marine designer, a shipwright, and a hydraulic engineer. Admiral Mitchell declined an invitation to command Peter's fleet, but helped him to recruit a Scottish mathematician, Dr. Farquharson, to teach navigation. For reasons that became clear later, Peter hired a pair of barbers. He also interviewed several mining engineers, but could not afford to pay the salaries they demanded.

Money was running low. The Tsar had made substantial

purchases of military and naval supplies, scientific instruments, books, specimens, and samples of all sorts. The salaries, living expenses, and travel costs of a growing army of foreigners were a new drain on his resources. He was inclined to listen when his friend Carmarthen made him a business proposition.

Carmarthen had friends in the tobacco trade who were eager to expand their markets. If Peter would offer them a monopoly on importing tobacco into Russia, they would pay him now a sum of ready money as an advance against future customs dues. The figure agreed upon was £12,000, or 28,000 rubles.

The bargain struck between the English Lord and the Russian Tsar on a yacht on the Thames was to have far-reaching consequences. Tobacco import duties would help to finance wars on the borders of Peter's huge domain. The increased demand for tobacco would spur Virginia and Maryland planters to bring more land under cultivation. The need for cheap labor would stimulate the trade in slaves from Africa to the American colonies. And profits from the sale of American tobacco and African slaves would swell the strongboxes of London merchants. Within a few decades, the tobacco monopoly Peter offered for an advance of £12,000 against duties was netting English merchants £120,000 annually.

Peter signed the contract with Carmarthen on April 26, 1698. Two days later, he had his farewell audience with King William. Despite their diplomatic differences, the two monarchs parted friends. Peter was taking away with him the King's yacht, sixty technical experts, and a vast quantity of arms and equipment. Even more important was the knowledge he had gained and the faith that he could apply it in Muscovy. When he boarded the *Royal Transport* to sail down the Thames, he had every reason to believe that his four months in England had been well spent.

Chapter 16

THE ROAD HOME

In Amsterdam, Peter found a small army of engineers, artisans, naval officers, and soldiers of fortune. There were more than 700 westerners bound for service in Muscovy, and so much equipment that he had to hire ten ships to carry passengers and cargo to Archangel.

The *Royal Transport* would sail with them. She was to be taken upstream from Archangel to Vologda, from which she would be hauled overland to the headwaters of the Volga River. Once the Don-Volga canal was finished, she could be sailed down the Volga to Azov, where Peter would command her in an attempt to open a way into the Black Sea.

First, he planned a trip to Vienna to revive Austrian interest in the war against Turkey. From there, he would go on to Venice to study the construction of galleys for use in the Black Sea. News that his Austrian and Venetian allies were listening to Turkish proposals for a peace conference alarmed him. He cut short his stay in Amsterdam and hurried to the Austrian capital.

His route took him across Saxony, whose ruler he had helped to elect King of Poland. King Augustus was abroad, but he sent orders to his ministers to gratify the Tsar's every whim. They did. On his first evening in Dresden, when it was already past midnight, Peter asked to visit the museum. He kept its curator talking until dawn. The next two evenings, he stayed up all night drinking and dancing with Augustus's beautiful mistress, then drove on, leaving his Saxon hosts to catch up on their sleep.

There was no such gaiety in Vienna, the seat of the slowest-moving court in Europe. It required many days and three separate petitions to arrange an informal meeting with Emperor Leopold, and then it lasted only a quarter of an hour. Despite his impatience, the Tsar was on his good behavior. Diplomatic observers commented on his "delicate and polished manners." But when he discussed matters with Count Kinsky, the Austrian foreign minister, he found his self-restraint had been in vain.

Kinsky proposed that peace with Turkey should be made on the principle that each of the allies could keep what it had conquered. This did not suit Peter at all. He had taken Azov, but the Turkish fortress of Kerch still blocked his way into the Black Sea. Kinsky pointed out that the peace conference could not begin for several months. If the Tsar wanted Kerch, all he had to do was take it before the conference. Knowing this to be impossible, Peter saw that he could expect no help from Austria.

He was preparing to move on to Venice when he received a letter from Romodanovsky, reporting a Streltsy uprising. Four regiments were marching on the capital, and were only sixty miles away. Shein and Gordon were advancing to meet them, but had not made contact at the time of writing. Peter wrote immediately: "We shall be with you sooner than you know." Four days later, with Lefort and Golovin, he galloped out of Vienna.

He had hardly departed when a second letter from Moscow reported that the rebellion was crushed. Peter was traveling with such speed that the courier sent after him did not overtake him until he was deep into Poland. For a moment Peter hesitated, then continued toward Moscow at a slower pace. On August 10, he paused in Rava for a fateful meeting with Augustus, the Saxon King of Poland.

The two monarchs had much in common. They were both young, tall, handsome, and powerful. Like Peter, Augustus could straighten a horseshoe with his bare hands. Like him, he drank heroically and dreamed of military glory. After a day of maneuvers, in which the Saxon troops impressed the Russian Tsar, the two young men sat up late, drinking. Peter had no way of knowing that his bluff companion was more at home in the boudoir than on the battlefield. He had dozens of mistresses and is said to have sired no fewer than three hundred illegitimate children. He lacked many of Peter's virtues—his energy, determination, self-discipline, and dauntlessness in defeat—but he captivated the Tsar at their first meeting, and the result was important. They planned a military alliance aimed not against Turkey, but against Sweden.

The idea of a league against Sweden was not new. Frederick of Prussia had suggested it to Peter more than a year before. Sweden was a traditional enemy of Russia, and war with her was quite as natural as war with Turkey. Therefore, although Peter's shift of direction from the Turkish-controlled Black Sea to the Swedish-controlled Baltic was as sudden as that from Archangel to Azov, it possessed the same inner consistency. He could not hope for English, Dutch, or Austrian support against Turkey. Now here was Augustus, with a splendid Saxon army, eager to help him against Sweden. He did not abandon his dream of a fleet on the Black Sea. He only postponed it in order to win his way into the Baltic. When he bade farewell and took the road for Moscow, his mind was seething with new possibilities.

It was good to return to the infinite spaciousness of Russian land and sky, but coupled with his pleasure with the familiar scenery, the comfortable sound of his native tongue, the homely taste of cabbage soup and black bread, was the pain of seeing more clearly than ever how backward his people were. With their shaggy hair and beards, their greasy sheepskins and leg wrappings, their bark sandals and rolling gait, they looked more like bears dressed up for a carnival than human beings.

Peter had learned much on his voyage of discovery. He was bringing back from the west plans and models, instruments and equipment, tools and technicians to recreate its likeness on Russian soil. Most important of all, he believed that progress was possible and that he could force his people to it.

His reliance on force has caused critics to conclude that Peter missed the real spirit of the west. He understood its technical skills and material achievements, but not its concept of constitutional government, its regard for the sanctity of person and property, and its respect for the dignity and worth of the individual human being. Yet western Europe at this time was less progressive and humanitarian than might be supposed. If Peter was autocratic he was hardly more so than Louis XIV. Every state on the continent permitted trial by torture, and even England, which did not, held public floggings and executions. In the maritime countries, press gangs seized free men and forced them into a brutal and dangerous sea service that often ended in death. The navies in which they fought were warring not for noble principles of justice and human freedom, but for colonies and commerce, including commerce in chained slaves.

Peter sometimes reflected the savagery of the Muscovite past, but he foreshadowed the future as well. He was unaware of the constitutional principles of the English revolution of 1688, but he instinctively grasped the philosophic basis of a future revolution. A century and a half later, Karl Marx would write, "The philosophers hitherto have only interpreted the world in various ways: the thing is, however, to change it."

Peter wanted to change his world, and if the barbarism of his methods recalled Ivan the Terrible, his faith in progress anticipated Marx and Lenin. Physically, Peter was a giant. Historically, he was a colossus, for he straddled four centuries of Russian history. When he drove into Moscow on September 4, 1698, he was twenty-six years old. Half his life was behind him. His revolution was about to begin.

BOOK THREE

War and Revolution

Chapter **17**

SALVATION BY CRUELTY

No one expected Peter so soon, and his arrival was almost furtive. He avoided the Kremlin and his wife Eudoxia, dropped Golovin and Lefort at their houses, called briefly on Anna Mons, and drove on to Preobrazhensky for the night. Nevertheless, the news of the Tsar's return spread rapidly.

Early next morning, the courtyard at Preobrazhensky began to fill with the carriages of great boyars and ministers. Coachmen swore and cracked their whips. Horses shook their bridles and tossed their long manes. Bearded magnates in embroidered caftans climbed the painted wooden steps of the palace and hurried to the audience chamber. More than once during the Tsar's absence, they had known panic at reports of his death. Their relief at seeing him now was overwhelming. They prostrated themselves at his feet, thanking God for his safe return.

Smiling, Peter raised them up and greeted each with a kiss. He was jovial and friendly to them all, even the

Patriarch, but there was an occasional gleam in his dark eyes. When he had welcomed the last arrival, he gave a little speech.

"You have tried to show your devotion and respect by flattening yourselves on your bellies, as if I were some barbarian Tartar khan. You would do me more honor to treat me like a civilized Christian monarch." His face twitched convulsively, and he began to pace. "If you love your Tsar, you should imitate his example. Look at me. Do I hide my face behind a great bush of whiskers like a heathen Turk? No! I shave it clean like the civilized Christian rulers of Europe—like all Christians everywhere but here in our unhappy Muscovy."

He paused, then laughed. "Hey, there, Shein!" His great hand shot out and closed on the long gray beard of his generalissimo. "What are you hiding behind this garden of weeds? Let me see the flower of thy face!"

A pair of scissors flashed in his other hand, and in a moment, he had cut off Shein's luxuriant beard close to the chin. There was a gasp of horror, but the Tsar's furious glare silenced protest. He called in his two English barbers. Then and there, he set them to work shaving off the beards of everyone present except the Patriarch and two of the oldest boyars.

When the great men, one by one, emerged into the pitiless light outside, their coachmen and servants were struck dumb. The boyars of all the greatest families of Muscovy were shorn like sheep. The skin of jowls so long protected from the sun and wind was unnaturally white. Its nakedness was hideous to behold.

When Shein gave a banquet a few days later, Peter arrived with his barbers dressed as jesters. The razoring was made part of the merrymaking, but Peter's humor was cruel, and his temper was erratic. Before five hundred guests, he accused Shein of selling commissions in the army, and although such sales were the accepted practice throughout Europe, he worked himself into a fury. He rushed from the room and returned with drawn sword. When he raised it to strike, Lefort managed to deflect the first blow, but Zotov was cut in the head, and Romodanovsky in the hand. Then Peter's mood suddenly changed. A few minutes later he was as cheerful as if nothing had happened, and kept the party going until dawn.

His sudden outbursts continued for weeks. No one was safe. Once he hurled Lefort to the floor and kicked him. Another time, he bloodied Menshikov's nose, because he was wearing his sword while dancing. Such attacks on his closest friends indicate tremendous nervous strain. He was being tormented by two problems. He wanted to end his marriage to Eudoxia, and he had to get to the bottom of the Streltsy uprising.

From England that spring, he had written to Lev Naryshkin and others urging them to persuade Eudoxia to go into a convent. This was the equivalent of divorce in the Russian Church. But the usually docile Eudoxia proved unexpectedly stubborn. She had no joy in her marriage, but she was devoted to her son Alexis. If she were shut up in a convent, she might never see him again.

This was just what Peter intended. His concern for Alexis was his real motive for putting Eudoxia away. Marriage did not hinder his personal freedom, and he needed no divorce to enjoy himself with Anna Mons or anyone else. Alexis was another matter. The eight-year-old Tsarevich was heir to the throne. Until now, Peter had ignored him.

Suddenly, he realized that the future of the new Russia he was planning would one day rest with his son. The boy would never learn to appreciate the advantages of westernization as long as he remained under the influence of his German-hating mother. She must be removed.

Soon after his return to Moscow, Peter sent for Eudoxia. Their interview lasted four hours. There is no record of what they said to each other, but three weeks later, Alexis was placed in the care of Peter's sister, Natalia. He was sent to live in Preobrazhensky and given a German tutor. The Tsaritsa Eudoxia was bundled into a common cart and driven to the Pokrovsky Convent in Suzdal.

By this time, Peter was already deeply absorbed in the investigation of the Streltsy revolt. His first thought had been: "The seed of Ivan Miloslavsky is sprouting." The uprising must be the work of an archenemy seeking to frustrate his grand design for the Russian people. Since he could no longer blame the dead Ivan Miloslavsky, Peter began to see his evil genius in feminine form. Sophia and only Sophia must be at the bottom of it. The investigation he launched was meant to prove a foregone conclusion. It was a witch-hunt, pure and simple.

The hunt began methodically. Fourteen torture chambers were constructed at Preobrazhensky. Each was assigned two scribes to write down the answers to certain questions, which Peter himself drew up. Romodanovsky was put in general charge. The interrogation began on September 27. A sergeant named Zorin broke on the first day. The Streltsy, he said, had planned to kill all foreigners, burn down the German Suburb, and petition Sophia to take the throne. The mention of Sophia was just what

Peter wanted, but he still had to prove that she had taken part in the plot.

Day after day, scores of Streltsy were put to torture. The questions of the scribes alternated with the whistle and crack of the knout, the groans and sobs of the victims, and the occasional stench of burning flesh, but no solid evidence turned up. At the report of a letter from Sophia to the rebels, her women servants and ladies-in-waiting were stripped to the waist and knouted like common soldiers, yet their confessions added nothing.

Peter decided to question Sophia in person. He stopped short of torture for a princess of the royal family, but on October 17, he drove to the nunnery. Their meeting was private. It must have resembled the confrontation in the Cathedral of the Assumption nine years before. He was still the handsome young wolf; she, the squat old bulldog. The bulldog was as defiant as ever. She admitted nothing. Peter failed to break her will, but he could break the only weapon she could use against him. He would destroy the Streltsy.

Two days later, the executions began. Five men were beheaded in Preobrazhensky, and 196 more were driven to Moscow and hanged in public places around the city. Within a month 1200 men were put to torture, and 799 were executed by hanging, beheading, and breaking on the wheel. Hundreds more would follow. Their bodies were left to swing in the wind or lie in frozen pools of blood throughout the winter. In the end, all the Streltsy in Moscow were disbanded. Their weapons, houses, and land were confiscated, and 16,000 men with their wives and children were exiled to distant parts of the country.

Sophia was forced to become a nun. Her head was shaved and her attendants taken from her. She was set under the guard of a hundred soldiers, whose instructions Peter wrote out in his own hand.

Neither Sophia nor the Streltsy were proved guilty as charged. Their punishment was entirely unjust, but it made sense to Peter. As long as the Streltsy were the armed guards of the capital, his program of westernization would be in

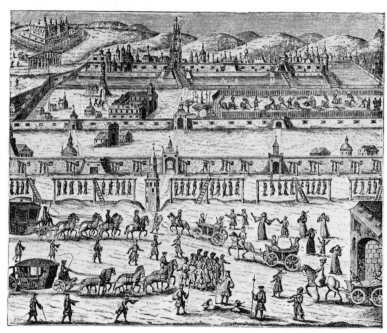

After the mass executions of the Streltsy, one of Peter's former admirers, Bishop Burnet, lamented that "so furious a man" should have such absolute authority over so many subjects; but violence was habitual in Muscovy. In the foreground, two women convicted of murder have been buried alive to die of thirst and starvation.

danger. Even the Austrian secretary, who was no admirer of Peter, seemed to justify him. "It had come to pass," he wrote, "that Muscovy was only to be saved by cruelty, not by pity."

Chapter 18

THE TSAR BEGINS
A REVOLUTION

When Peter interrupted his homecoming audience to shear off Generalissimo Shein's beard, he signaled the beginning of a revolution. His attack on beards was based on a radical new concept of the state. The absolute authority of the Tsar had been growing for centuries, and there was no institution or class that could oppose it, yet the power of the autocracy was limited. It was limited not by law, but by custom.

Custom played a major role in the life of the people. Over the years there had been many changes in Muscovy, but they had come about so gradually that it was easy to believe life was still going on in the same old way. There were wars, invasions, uprisings, plagues, and famines, but when they passed, the people went back to the customs of their ancestors. The Tsar could and did sponsor changes in institutions, but he seldom interfered in the private lives of his subjects, or, if he did, it was on the side of custom and against change.

There had been one notable exception to this rule. When Tsar Alexis had supported the reforms of the Patriarch Nikon, he had attacked custom and sponsored change in the most sensitive area of Muscovite life—religion. When Peter began to shave his courtiers, he was, in a sense, renewing his father's battle with the Old Believers and affirming the Tsar's right to regulate the private life of the people. Beards were sacred. They had been given to men by God to distinguish them from the lower animals. "Nothing but the absolute authority of the Tsar," wrote John Perry, an English engineer in Peter's service, "could ever have prevailed with the Russes to have parted with their beards." Peter claimed such authority: "His Majesty is absolute monarch who need not answer for his acts to anyone in the world, but has power and authority as a Christian sovereign to govern his states and lands according to his will and his benevolent understanding." It was his benevolent understanding that beards were the sign of a backward Asiatic people, and it was his will to eliminate them.

Perry described the Voronezh workmen's reaction to the shaving. When he jokingly asked one of them what he had done with his beard, "he put his hand in his bosom and pulled it out, and showed it to me: further telling me, that when he came home, he would lay it up to have it put in his coffin and buried along with him, that he might be able to give an account of it to St. Nicholas when he came to the other world."

Peter tried to turn such superstition to his advantage by establishing a beard tax. It ranged from one sixth of a kopeck a year for a peasant to one hundred rubles a year for a rich merchant. As receipts for payment, they were issued bronze tokens to wear around their necks like dog licenses. Courtiers, officials, army officers, and soldiers were forced to shave, but the vast majority of merchants and peasants, and all monks and priests, kept their beards.

Peter used similar methods in ordering his people to give up their Muscovite costumes. Devout believers felt it would be sacrilege to worship in a Russian church dressed

The Bettmann Archive

Peter's shaving the beards of his boyars captured the imagination of contemporaries. A cartoonist shows him brandishing his scissors and grinning, while his intended victim protests.

like a German heretic. The Tsar ordered all members of the court or persons in government service to wear western dress. He had samples of such clothes hung up on all the gates of the city of Moscow and commanded that all the inhabitants except common peasants should have their clothes made like them. Nobles and merchants entering the capital in their caftans either were fined or had their skirts cut off at the knees.

The Tsar's "revolution" had its limits. He lacked the practical power to force all the millions in his vast country to change their ways. Only courtiers or those in government service came within his effective reach. They obeyed him and, in appearance at least, followed him into eighteenth-century Europe. Peasants, merchants, and churchmen remained in the Asiatic past.

Peter could argue that western clothes were more practical than flowing robes, but convenience was not his sole object. Shaving was a nuisance, not a convenience. Peter disliked beards and caftans as remnants of the Mongol period. To make his people behave like Europeans, he wanted them to look like Europeans. His reasoning was naive, but the effect was valuable as a kind of discipline. The courtiers and officials he forced to shave were daily reminded of the Tsar's authority over them. They could not forget that they were wearing their new foreign clothes by his order. Their razored cheeks and western dress set them apart from the people and proclaimed them as the Tsar's men employed on the Tsar's business.

Peter's revolution was more radical for women than for men. His sister Natalia set the fashion of wearing western costume, but the change in the women's dress style was less important than the change in their life style. The Tsar who confined his own wife to a convent freed the wives of his nobles from the confinement of the terem. He ordered that "at all weddings and all other public entertainments, the women as well as the men should be invited . . . and that they should be entertained in the same room with the men, like as he had seen in foreign countries, and that the evening should be concluded with music and dancing."

Westernization meant modernization, and in his reform of the calendar, Peter brought Russia up to date in the literal sense. The old calendar numbered the years from the creation of the world, rather than from the birth of Christ. The year was 7207, rather than 1699. The year began in September, because God would not have created man in the depth of winter, when there was nothing to eat, but in harvest time, when fruit and grain were ripe. Peter decreed that a western calendar should go into effect on January 1, 1700; but his reform was not complete.

Since 46 B.C., most of Europe had been using the calendar introduced by Julius Caesar, but the Julian year was eleven minutes longer than the astronomic year, and over the centuries, the discrepancy resulted in a cumulative loss of days. In 1582, Pope Gregory XII attempted to correct the error by adding ten days to his calendar, but Protestant countries refused to accept it, because it was Catholic. England did not finally adopt the Gregorian calendar until 1752. Up to that time, as Voltaire remarked, the English preferred to disagree with the sun rather than agree with the Pope. Peter shared England's anti-Catholic bias and he adopted the Julian calendar.

As in so many of his reforms, Peter combined the calendar change with a public celebration. He could publicize innovations and make them more acceptable at festive gatherings enlivened with liquor and laughter. He decreed special New Year's services in all the churches, bonfires and fireworks in the Red Square, and seven days of public feasting.

On January 6, the Feast of the Epiphany, he interrupted his revels to attend the blessing of the waters by the Patriarch. Spectators crowded rooftops and the walls of the Kremlin. The sun glittered on the brocade and gemencrusted headdresses of five hundred church dignitaries. Swinging smoking censers, holding lighted candles, and chanting in unison, they advanced on a red carpet spread across the ice to a pavilion decorated with ikons. Here, a hole had been chopped in the ice, so that Adrian could bless the waters supposed at that moment to be mystically transformed into the waters of the River Jordan.

Instead of sitting beside Adrian on his throne, Peter stood at the head of his Guards. There were 12,000 troops, wearing new green uniforms and black tricorn hats. When the ceremony was over, they raised their English muskets and fired three times at the command of the Tsar.

The scene was a curious blend of the old and new. With its new calendar, Muscovy had entered the last year of the 17th century. The Patriarch would die before it was over. The flowing beards and Byzantine robes of the church fathers belonged to the eastern past. The shaven faces and German uniforms of the troops reflected a Russia turning west. This was the dawn of a new era.

Chapter 19

THE ROAD TO WAR

The presence of the troops at the blessing of the waters was a reminder that Peter was preparing for war with Sweden. These preparations were less colorful than his attacks on beards and native costumes, but they were to have deep and lasting consequences both at home and abroad.

Peter shared the preoccupation of western statesmen with war and trade, but since he lacked an adequate seaport through which to trade, he began with war. Trade was the end, but war was the means to that end, and war had to come first. Moreover, war involved many supporting programs. The war with Turkey had led to the construction of a fleet at Voronezh, work on a Don-Volga canal, and the launching of the Great Embassy. War with Sweden would require peace with Turkey, the creation of a new army, and the raising of taxes to support that army. To function effectively in war, a variety of nonmilitary gears and cogwheels had to be set in motion.

After the first wave of Streltsy executions in the fall of 1698, Peter drove off to Voronezh to inspect his navy. A score of ships had been launched, and as many more were on their way to completion. Before the trip abroad, he would have been overjoyed, but his months in the dockyards of Amsterdam and Deptford had sharpened his critical eye. He could see that the workmanship was shoddy, the materials defective, and the designs a mismating of the conflicting national traditions of the western shipwrights. Staring out at his mongrel fleet frozen in the river under a leaden November sky, he expressed his misgivings in a letter. "A cloud of doubt covers my mind whether I shall ever taste of these fruits, or whether they be like dates, which those that plant them never gather."

The remedy for doubt was work. He laid down the keel of a new ship, ordered the rebuilding and refitting of others, and revived his spirits with labor in the open air. Returning to the capital refreshed for the Christmas holidays, he looked to his finances. An anonymous letter dropped in one of the Kremlin offices suggested a new form of taxation, requiring all formal documents, contracts, or agreements to be written on stamped paper purchased from the government. Peter adopted this Muscovite version of the Stamp Act and tracked down its anonymous author. He proved to be a former serf named Kurbatov. Peter appointed him the first of a new class of officials called "profit makers." Their duty was to think up ways to increase government revenue. In effect, they devised extortionate new taxes.

This was typical of many so-called reforms of the period. Peter had neither the time nor the temperament to thoroughly rebuild the antiquated machinery of the Muscovite state. Instead, he tinkered with it. He forged, welded, patched, and mended. He invented new parts or adapted old ones to new uses. He improvised as he went along, and his reforms often fell short of the mark. For example, he removed the collection of many taxes from his corrupt military governors and gave it to town councils elected by the merchants. This was a temporary improvement, but the merchants soon became nearly as corrupt as the military governors.

In the week before Lent, Peter arranged a perfect orgy of feasting to dedicate a new palace he had given Franz Lefort. On the dawn following the last night, he said good-bye to his favorite and drove away to Voronezh. In March, he had word that Lefort was seriously ill. He died before Peter could reach his side. Grief-stricken, the Tsar sobbed, "Now I am left without one friend I can trust!"

This was near the truth. As supreme autocrat, Peter could have no real friends, because he had no real equals; but Lefort had come close. He had shared Peter's enthusiasms and encouraged his ambitions. He was both honest and unselfish. All Peter's Russian favorites heaped up vast fortunes by corruption. Lefort lived in princely style, but he died nearly as poor as when he had come to Russia.

Following the funeral, Peter conceived of a bizarre dip-lomatic venture. The negotiations with Turkey had brought a two-year truce, but he was determined to have full peace in the south before launching a war against Sweden in the north. He appointed as his ambassador to Turkey an ex-perienced privy councillor and made plans to send him to Constantinople in a Russian man-of-war. He and the entire Voronezh fleet would convoy it down the Don and force a passage through the Turkish-held Straits of Kerch.

It took two months in the dockyards to ready the fleet. There were 18 men-of-war and 139 ships and barges. Except for Captain Peter's, all the men-of-war were commanded by foreigners. They arrived in Azov in time for the celebration of the Tsar's twenty-seventh birthday, June 9, 1699. Later, at Taganrog, the entire fleet had to be careened and recaulked before it could continue. It was late August when at last it swooped down on Kerch, firing its guns in salute.

The Turkish commander was thunderstruck. He had no choice but to grant Peter's demand for passage. Early in September, the *Fortress*, a 46-gun frigate commanded by a Dutch captain, became the first Russian warship to sail the Black Sea in more than four centuries. Ten days later, it dropped anchor under the very walls of the Sultan's palace. It caused a sensation, but it had diverted Peter's attention from raising the new army for six precious months.

Returning to Moscow, the Tsar found two foreign delegations awaiting him. One was seeking peace. The other was planning for war. An embassy from Charles XII, the new King of Sweden, requested confirmation of a longstanding treaty with Russia. Peter had already confirmed it once sixteen years before, but now it guaranteed to Sweden the Baltic provinces that he and Augustus were planning to conquer. Feeling the awkwardness of his position, the Tsar delayed as long as he dared, but finally reconfirmed the treaty he had every intention of breaking.

During these discussions, councils of war were going on at Preobrazhensky. The most fiery advocate for immediate action was Baron Patkul, a Livonian nobleman who had taken service with Augustus and who burned to free his country of Swedish rule. He had a plan to solve Augus-

tus's problem in Poland. In Saxony, where he was hereditary ruler, Augustus could declare war at will, but in Poland, where he was elected, he needed the consent of the
native nobility. Patkul insisted that the Saxon army could
easily take Riga by surprise, and that this was sure to bring
the Polish nobility into the war behind their Saxon King.
He urged Peter to invade Swedish holdings farther north
at the same time. But Peter was not prepared. Thanks to
his Black Sea adventure, he had only begun recruiting his
new army. Besides, he insisted on peace with Turkey as
a condition of war with Sweden.

The Tsar's deliberations were interrupted by the loss of
an old friend and adviser. General Gordon's health had
been failing for some time. Now it took a turn for the
worse. At his deathbed, Peter held a mirror to the old Scot's
mouth for a sign of breath. When there was none, he
closed the dead man's eyes with his own hands. He missed
Gordon as a friend. He would miss him even more as a
general.

Recruits for the new army were pouring into Preobrazhensky. They lumbered into camp—great shaggy fellows
in birchbark shoes. They were shaved and barbered to improve their military appearance and to insure prompt detection of any who deserted. They were dressed in smart
uniforms and boots. Their English flintlocks were much
less likely to misfire than the old wheel locks, and they
were equipped with a new type of French bayonet. Instead
of fitting into the mouth of the barrel, this new bayonet
left the muzzle clear. A soldier could fire his musket and
stab with his bayonet at one and the same time. Twenty-
nine regiments were raised during the winter, and on the
drill field they impressed foreign observers.

Warfare required money as well as men and material. The weakness of Russian coinage hindered the collection of taxes, and Peter needed taxes to pay for English flintlocks, French bayonets, and German uniforms. The only coins in circulation were silver kopecks, which were cut into pieces to make small change. Better coins, and coins of both larger and smaller denominations, were needed. Peter personally supervised the operation of the Mint. It began turning out copper coins for small change, and later minted silver coins as well. It produced nine million rubles in its first three years, and they were an important asset to both war and trade.

The war against Sweden had been scheduled to begin on Christmas Day, 1699, with a surprise attack on Riga by the Saxon army. It opened like a bad comic opera. Rather, it failed to open, for when the curtain rose, none of the principals were on stage. Peter was in Preobrazhensky waiting for peace with Turkey. Augustus was in Dresden, disporting himself with his mistress. Charles XII was in Stockholm, suspecting no treachery. General Flemming, the Saxon commander, had suddenly taken it into his head to get married and left the army without giving the order to attack. When he returned in February, he found that it had not budged. In the meantime, Governor General Dahlberg had got wind of the attack and had so strengthened the defenses of Riga that an assault without siege artillery was unthinkable. The entire plan was aborted.

As spring turned to summer in 1700, Peter made secret plans to invade the Baltic provinces of Ingria and Karelia and quietly moved troops to Pskov and Novgorod. He was encouraged by the news that Denmark had invaded Holstein, an ally of Sweden. He sent an envoy to Frederick of Prussia to entice him into the war. All the time, he was lying shamelessly to the Swedish Ambassador, promising eternal peace and friendship.

On August 19, word came that Peter's ambassador to Turkey had concluded peace with the Sultan in Constantinople. Russia kept Azov and Taganrog, but Turkey continued to hold Kerch and the straits to the Black Sea. The next day, August 20, 1700, Peter declared war on Sweden and set off for the frontier, unaware that he was taking the road to disaster.

Chapter 20

NARVA

There was good reason for supposing that Sweden was vulnerable. Her extended frontiers around the Baltic were difficult to defend. Denmark, Saxony, and Russia were allied against her, and it seemed probable that Poland and Prussia would soon join them. Finally, since 1697, the Swedish throne had been occupied by a mere boy—and a headstrong boy at that.

At fifteen, Charles had refused a coronation. He held that coronations were proper only for elective monarchies like that of Poland. He had been born to the crown, and on the ceremonial day, he went to the church already wearing it. What followed was not a coronation, but a consecration, in which the Archbishop confirmed him as "the Anointed of the Lord." It was marred at the climax when the Archbishop dropped the anointing oil, and the crown the arrogant youth had placed on his own head fell to the floor with a clatter.

Like Peter, Charles showed an early interest in military

exercises. Unlike him, he had a passion for exposing himself to physical danger. Having decided that it was cowardly to use firearms for bear hunting, he soon abandoned even pikes and cutlasses. Members of his hunting party were armed with long wooden forks. They were supposed to catch the charging bear under the throat and throw him on his back, so that the huntsmen could spring forward and cover the animal with a net. Reckless horsemanship nearly cost him his life more than once. His compulsion to prove his courage was suicidal. Unable to swim, he jumped overboard during a sham naval battle and nearly drowned.

He shunned the company of women and went to extremes to toughen his body. He often slept on the floor in a shirt. He ate only coarse food and drank neither wine nor any other liquor. In the summer of 1698, when Charles was 16, Frederick of Holstein-Gottorp came to Stockholm to marry Charles's sister, and the two young men went on a rampage that became known as the "Holstein frenzy." They rode horses to death. They loosed a hare and hounds in the Senate. They smashed dinner plates and glasses and threw furniture from the palace windows. They ordered sheep, goats, dogs, and cats brought to the royal apartments and practiced their swordsmanship by beheading them. For days, the floors and stairs ran red with blood. Yet this cruel, arrogant, and harebrained youth possessed a kind of military genius.

Peter had his first inkling of this on his way to lay siege to Narva. In Tver, he learned that Charles had invaded Denmark so unexpectedly that the Danes had surrendered without a battle. This in turn had frightened Prussia into strict neutrality, and Charles was soon expected to land in Pernau with 18,000 men. Peter hesitated, then moved on toward Narva with the Guards.

The fall rains had softened the roads to mire. The light peasant carts commandeered by the army continually broke down under the weight of military cargo. Peter did not reach Narva until late September. The city stood on the bank of the Narva River ten miles from the Baltic Sea. Both it and the fortress of Ivangorod across the river were strongly walled, and until the siege artillery could be brought up, there was nothing to do but build ramparts and trenches.

In mid-October, the divisions of Generals Weide and Golovin arrived with the heavy artillery. A Saxon engineer directed the placing of the batteries, and the bombardment began, but the results were disheartening. Russian gunpowder was unreliable. Many shots misfired or fell far short. The recoils from these harmless cannonades shattered many gun carriages. After two weeks, without having made a single breach in the walls, the ammunition gave out and the guns fell silent. An attempt to storm the fortress of Ivangorod was repulsed, with heavy losses. A garrison of only 1500 Swedes was keeping an army of 30,000 Russians at bay.

There was ominous news from the south. Charles had landed at Pernau and was advancing with an army reported between 30,000 and 32,000 men. Peter dispatched General Sheremetev with 5,000 cavalry to make contact. Morale in the Russian camp was low. Surprise sorties by the Swedes inflicted casualties and showed their superiority as soldiers. A foreign Guards officer who had been a favorite of Peter's deserted to the enemy. General Sheremetev reported that he was falling back before Charles. On November 29, Peter turned over the command to the Duke von Croy and left for Moscow.

Von Croy was a foreigner who spoke no Russian and was unknown to the Russian generals under his command. Peter's abandonment of him on the very eve of battle may seem a flight from both personal responsibility and physical danger, but no one imagined that Charles could move with such lightning speed. The Tsar could reasonably have assumed that von Croy had time to prepare his defenses.

A number of concerns claimed Peter's attention in the rear but they do not explain his departure. For two months he had been watching his raw recruits in the field. He had seen cannon misfire, gun carriages splinter, and ammunition run out. Man for man, his troops were no match for the Swedes, and if he believed reports on the size of Charles's army, defeat must have seemed inevitable. He was wise enough to accept that Narva was a battle he could lose, but if he were not to lose the war, he had to protect himself. It was common sense to leave the combat area.

He left not a moment too soon. Only hours later, General Sheremetev rode into camp with the news that the Swedes were only six miles off. They had been marching under frightful conditions. For eighty miles, the road ran through bogs and marshlands, and freezing mud that sucked up to the soldiers' ankles. Charles had abandoned the heavy baggage, and the troops had been practically without food for two days. Only iron discipline and the fiery will of their commander kept them going.

The battle of Narva began on November 30 at eleven

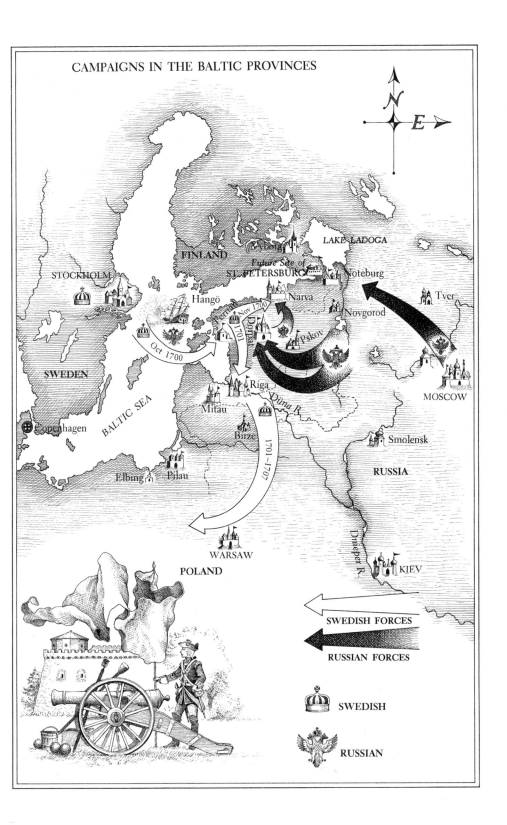

CAMPAIGNS IN THE BALTIC PROVINCES

N
E

STOCKHOLM

FINLAND

Vyborg

LAKE LADOGA

Future Site of
ST. PETERSBURG

Noteburg

Hangö

Narva

Tver

Oct 1700

Nov 1700

Dorpat

Novgorod

Pskov

SWEDEN

MOSCOW

Riga

BALTIC SEA

Mitau

Düna R.

Birze

Copenhagen

1701–1707

Smolensk

RUSSIA

Elbing

Pilau

WARSAW

POLAND

Dnieper R.

KIEV

SWEDISH FORCES

RUSSIAN FORCES

SWEDISH

RUSSIAN

o'clock in the morning. Von Croy believed that the Swedes who emerged from the covering woods were only the advance guard of a much larger force. In fact, 8,000 Swedes were attacking 30,000 Russians, but 4,000 of these were across the river surrounding Ivangorod, and the rest were strung out along a seven-mile line. The compactly-massed Swedes had numerical superiority at the point of their attack. To add to the confusion that always obscures events on a battlefield, at two o'clock a blinding snow squall covered the action. It whipped the white flakes so violently into the faces of the Russians that they could not see twenty feet. There were shouts, shots, the screaming of wounded horses, confused shapes in the white blur. According to the Saxon General Hallart, "The Russians ran about like a herd of cattle, one regiment mixed up with another, so that hardly twenty men could be got into line."

Sheremetev's cavalry were the first to break and run. They plunged into the Narva River above the cataracts. More than 1,000 men and 2,000 horses were drowned. Upstream, so many fleeing Russians crowded onto a bridge that it collapsed beneath them. When the foreign officers tried to rally the troops, a cry went up that the "Germans" had betrayed them. Blinded by snow, fear, and hatred, the Russians turned against the foreigners within their ranks, and several officers were killed. Fearing more from the Russians than the Swedes, von Croy and a number of others spurred their horses through the gathering darkness to surrender. The demoralized Russian generals followed suit.

Though the Russians did not know it, Charles's position was still precarious. His troops were exhausted. They had scarcely eaten or slept for days. "Besides this," one of their colonels wrote, "all our men were drunk with the brandy they had found in the Muscovite tents, so it was impossible for the few officers that remained to keep them in order." A determined counterattack by the Russian units that had not yet been committed might have turned the tide; but having no idea of the real state of the Swedish force, they came to terms.

For Charles, it was a magnificent victory. With a loss of 2,000 men, he had killed 8,000 Russians and routed an army nearly four times the size of his own. He had captured ten generals, ten colonels, scores of junior officers, immense stores, and 150 cannon. Flushed with victory, the young king ordered a commemorative medal that made Peter look ridiculous as it circulated through the courts of Europe. It showed the Tsar in flight, throwing away his sword, losing his hat, and holding a handkerchief to eyes spurting huge tears.

Peter might well have wept. He had lost his new army, his foreign generals, the whole of his artillery, and a great part of his reputation. The work of years had been wiped out in a few hours. Alexander Gordon wrote, "On hearing of the defeat and disaster of his army, the Tsar was much struck at first, but recollecting himself said, 'I know very well, the Swedes will for some time beat us, but at length, we may learn to beat them.'"

Chapter 21

WAR AND PROGRESS

The long-range effects of the Northern War were paradoxical. It imposed a staggering burden on the Russian people, and it was a principal stimulus to the modernization of the Russian state. But in the first days after Narva, Peter had no time to think of long-range effects. Emergency measures came first.

In Novgorod and Pskov, men, women, and children were put to work digging trenches. Prince Repnin was appointed to regroup the disorganized troops streaming eastward from the battle. Within two weeks, he had formed them into regiments totaling 22,000 men. Raw military manpower posed no problem. Armament was quite another matter.

Returning to Moscow, Peter appointed Andrew Vinius to the crucial task of replacing his lost artillery. Vinius was the son of the Dutch merchant who had built the iron works at Tula. To provide him with metal, Peter ordered all the towns, churches, and monasteries to contribute bells to be melted down. The decree produced 1,450 tons of bell metal, but bell metal alone was not strong enough for cannon. Iron would have to be added, and to provide it, ore would have to be mined and smelted. And after the cannon had been cast, they would have to be mounted on gun carriages.

Peter's greatest need was for time. After Narva, Charles had gone into winter quarters near Dorpat, but he would emerge in the spring, and it would take far more than one winter to rebuild and rearm Peter's shattered forces. There was only one way he could gain the necessary respite. He must encourage his ally Augustus to divert Charles with his well-trained Saxon army. Peter sent to Augustus to assure him of Russia's determination to continue the war. In February, he left Moscow to confer with him in Birze.

By pressing hard, the Tsar obtained a renewal of their agreement to fight to the bitter end. He had to pay an exorbitant price for it. He agreed to send Repnin with 20,000 troops to support the Saxon army outside Riga— Repnin's force represented a full half of Russia's regulars —and to augment the loan of troops with grants of money. He promised annual subsidies of 100,000 rubles for two years, and he added another 20,000 rubles to bribe the Polish magnates to join the war. To find the necessary money, he had to empty the coffers of every government department and even get contributions from wealthy individuals.

But all this would have been in vain if Charles had taken the advice of his counselors to march on Moscow in the spring. Without cannon, the capital was defenseless. Luckily for Peter, the nineteen-year-old Charles viewed the war as a personal conflict. He had been betrayed by three scoundrels. He had already humbled the Danish King and the Russian Tsar. Now he would settle with Augustus. In the spring of 1701, he turned his back on Moscow and marched south. Falling on the Saxon army outside Riga, he won a spectacular victory. Again, his generals reminded him that Moscow was his for the taking, but Charles preferred to pursue the Saxons into Poland. There he won one victory after another, but the war dragged on. He would be bogged down in Poland for six long years. This was the time Peter so desperately needed.

The Tsar saw clearly that the Swedes were superior to the Russians in everything but numbers. In discipline, organization, equipment, technology, and military science, Muscovy was way behind. To catch up, Peter would have to modernize not only the army, but the nation. He must do in a few years what had taken the west centuries to achieve.

Western warfare had changed radically with advances in artillery and engineering. Military progress was a product of science, and warfare stimulated scientific progress. The English Royal Society, founded in 1662, and the French Academy of Sciences, in 1666, conducted investigations into the chemistry of gunpowder, metallurgy, ballistics, the impact of projectiles, the recoil of cannon, and the improvement of navigation.

Because the Russians lacked technical and scientific training, Peter turned his attention to education. At first, he hoped that the old Slavonic Greek–Latin Academy could add mathematics and science to its religious studies. He had discussed the matter with Patriarch Adrian, but Adrian died while Peter was at Narva. In 1701, the Tsar made a new beginning. Instead of trying to combine scientific and religious training in the same institution, he founded a School of Mathematical and Navigational Sciences as a separate entity and put the Scottish mathematician Dr. Farquharson in charge. It was the first purely scientific and technical school in Russia, and it set the pattern for schools of artillery and engineering that followed.

War was as great a stimulus to industry as to education. Muskets and cannon required iron mines, gun foundries, and powder mills. Fleets had to be rigged and fitted. Armies and navies must be clothed in uniforms. In the advanced western countries, the state awarded loans, subsidies, and special privileges to private companies that supplied military needs. In backward Muscovy, where private industry was so much less developed, the state had to play a much larger role.

Peter created war industry on a vast scale. Before Narva, he had purchased flintlocks in England. Now he began to manufacture them at home. In 1701, Russia produced 6,000 flintlocks. By 1707, the output was 30,000. From 1701 to 1704, seven new iron works were opened in the Urals, and Russian mines and factories were on a scale that dwarfed those in western Europe. The nine mines of Perm had 25,000 miners. The Tula arms works employed the labor of 500 households. There were more than 1,000 hands in the Moscow sail factory.

Working conditions were harsh, and workers were little more than industrial slaves, but Peter got results. In 1700, Russia was the least-developed of the great powers. By 1718, her iron production exceeded 100,000 tons a year, many times that of England.

The new army had to be trained as well as equipped. The

various branches had to be taught special skills, and their separate functions had to be coordinated through a disciplined chain of command. The famous report of the ex-peasant Pososhkov shows how far Peter's army was from this ideal in 1701:

"The infantry are armed with bad muskets and do not know how to use them. They fight with their sidearms, with lances and halberds, and even these are blunt; for every foreigner killed, there are three, four, or even more Russians killed. As for the cavalry, we are ashamed to look at them ourselves, let alone show them to the foreigner— sickly ancient horses, blunt sabers, puny badly-dressed men who do not know how to wield their weapons."

With officers like Weide, Bruce, and Menshikov, Peter began to whip this unpromising material into a modern army. Discipline was severe. The term of service was lengthened to twenty-five years. Over such a time, peasant soldiers lost their ties with their native villages and began to think of their regiment as their home and of soldiering as their career. They became expert in the handling of their weapons, and the Russian army was the first in history to employ the bayonet charge as a decisive offensive maneuver.

Pososhkov's report had said of the officers, "They care nothing for killing the enemy, but think only of how to return to their homes. They pray that God will send them a light wound, so as not to suffer much, for which they will receive a reward from their sovereign. In battle, they hide in thickets. Whole companies take cover in a forest or a valley."

To create a professional officer class, Peter hammered away at the idea that promotion depended on merit and length of service, rather than on personal favor or family connections. He dramatized this concept in his own life. As a boy, even though he was the crowned Tsar, he had enrolled himself as a common soldier in the play regiments and worked his way up through the ranks. He never permitted himself a promotion he had not earned, and he staged each promotion as a public ceremony. Romodanovsky or another of his companions played the role of Mock Tsar. The Mock Tsar addressed him by his new title as Bombardier Peter or Captain Peter, complimenting him on the particular service that had earned him this promotion and promising further advancement, if he continued to deserve it.

Peter was an elaborate joker, and he enjoyed these ceremonies, but they had none of the buffoonery of the All Drunken Synod, and any resemblance is strictly superficial. The Tsar was in earnest. Each promotion was based on real achievement. His professional competence was stressed, and his salary was delivered in the presence of all. He was seeking to implant the ideals of a responsible, professionally trained, and salaried state service in the minds of a generally irresponsible, untrained, and self-seeking nobility. The pattern was later applied to civil administration, but it was first worked out in the army. It was one more way in which the challenge of a modern war accelerated the progress of Muscovy from a medieval to a modern state.

Chapter 22

THE FOUNDING
OF ST. PETERSBURG

Peter taught that the Russian state was more important than the person of the Tsar, but, in practice, his personality permeated the state. He was the incarnation of the new Russia. His character was stamped on every reform. As Alexander Pushkin, the great Russian poet, put it, he made Russia "rear like a stallion," and he seemed to be everywhere at once. The capital was no longer the Great Hall in the Kremlin. It was a military camp in Livonia, a hut on the banks of the Neva, the dockyards at Voronezh, or wherever the Tsar chanced to be.

According to the historian Klyuchevsky, "The government's most important and terrible weapon was Peter's pen. His immense correspondence with those responsible for the execution of current affairs covered every aspect of government. These letters took the place of laws. Their recipients became departments of state. Because of military requirements, the administration was turned into a military headquarters."

With Charles XII far away in Poland, Peter set to work on his frontier. In June, 1701, he appointed Sheremetev Commander in Chief in the West. An experienced general under Peter's father, Sheremetev had the respect of both the conservatives and those who saw the need for remodeling the army along western lines. He sometimes lacked initiative or determination, but Peter had more than enough of both. Under his prodding, the Russians won a series of minor engagements in Livonia.

In September, a Russian force wiped out a Swedish detachment of 300. In December, Sheremetev overwhelmed the army of Schlippenbach, killing 3,000 of the 8,000 Swedes and taking 350 prisoners. In the summer of 1702, he cleared Livonia of Swedes except for the garrisons of Riga, Dorpat, and Narva.

Early in October, Peter joined Sheremetev and Apraxin to lay siege to the small fortress of Noteburg on Lake Ladoga. Noteburg was named for the nutlike shape of the island on which it was built, and Peter punned to Vinius, "This nut was tough, but praise God, we have truly cracked it. Our artillery carried out its work magnificently." When the Swedish commandant surrendered the key, Peter nailed it over the main gate and renamed the fortress Schlüsselburg or Keyfort, because he regarded it as the key to the conquest of Ingria and the trade of the Baltic. Even before the victory banquet, he wrote seven letters proclaiming the recovery of a "national fortress."

As a military feat, the capture of Schlüsselburg was insignificant; but Peter grasped its vital strategic importance. He had a commemorative medal made. He arranged a triumphal entry into Moscow. He founded the first Russian newspaper to publicize it. He even commissioned a group of German players to stage an allegory of the victory in the Red Square.

After the customary Christmas festivities, Peter went down to Voronezh, where his good humor turned to anger. Hundreds of forced laborers had fled. Those who remained were ravaged by disease. Work was at a standstill. Worst of all, the ships that had already been finished were falling into decay, and their timbers were so warped and rotten that they could not stand the strain of careening for repairs. An Englishman improvised a sort of drydock that enabled the necessary repairs to be made without careening, but Peter was galled by his countrymen's lack of initiative. If he had not been there, they would have allowed fifteen ships simply to rot in the river.

When he returned to Schlüsselburg in March, he met with further frustration. The usually reliable and energetic Vinius had failed to supply the artillery for the conquest of Ingria. Having grown wealthy through profiteering in iron, he had fallen into indolence. Peter wrote to Romodanovsky in a fury. He was to examine Vinius at once and make it clear that the artillery was "a thousand times more important than his head." In the end, Vinius, who had been one of Peter's most capable lieutenants, was fined, knouted, and stripped of his offices.

Peter compensated for the loss of Vinius with new gains in Ingria. With Sheremetev, he took a small Swedish fortress on the Neva River, and when two unsuspecting Swedish vessels dropped anchor nearby, he and Menshikov rowed out with two Guards regiments under cover of darkness and overpowered their crews. On the same river where Alexander Nevsky had crushed the Swedes in 1240, Peter won his first naval victory over their descendants. After nearly five centuries the Neva had been restored to Mother Russia.

Neva derives from the Finnish word for mud. At the mouth of the river, deposits of silt had piled up nineteen low-lying islands dividing the main stream into four channels. Except for a few fishing huts, the islands were deserted. Waterfowl nested in the reeds. Long-legged wading birds stalked through mosquito-infested marshes. Few trees grew, and the sodden landscape was monotonously flat. But Peter saw it in the context of history. In the great days of Novgorod, the Neva had been an outlet for Russian trade into the Baltic. On May 27, 1703, shortly before his thirty-first birthday, he chose an island on the northern side of the main channel and laid out the plan of a fortress to defend a new city. It was to be named for his patron saint, St. Peter.

Construction began at once. Workmen were drafted from Novgorod. Tools, supplies, and even timber had to be brought from the interior. There were no roads, and transport across the marshy ground was difficult. But the Tsar was determined. He had a hut built for himself. There were only three small rooms and no stove, but the outside walls were painted to resemble brick, and the mica windows gave a view of the water. To Peter it was as good as a palace.

In July he took steps to increase his "city's" security. Striking north with the Guards twenty miles over terrain the Swedes had imagined impassable, he attacked a force of 4,000 at dawn. The surprise and fury of the Russian assault put the Swedes to flight. They left 1,000 dead to only 32 Russians.

Two weeks later, Peter was on the shore of Lake Ladoga,

where he had already established a dockyard for the construction of a Baltic fleet. When he had completed and rigged a frigate, he brought it down to St. Petersburg. In October, as soon as the Swedish fleet in the Gulf of Finland had retired for the winter, he sailed from the ice-rimmed mouth of the Neva to explore. Eight miles out in the gulf, he circled the island of Kotlin. Posting himself in the bow chains, he took soundings with the lead and found that there was sufficient depth to accommodate large warships. A fortress built on this island could protect St. Petersburg from attack by sea. He would name it Kronstadt.

Even before work on Kronstadt could begin, there was a good omen. A Dutch merchant ship, blown off course, was sighted in the gulf. Peter sailed out and personally piloted

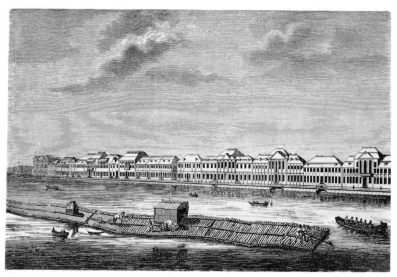

Building materials for St. Petersburg had to be brought from far in the interior of Russia. Here logs for pilings and timber have been lashed together and floated down the Neva River as huge rafts.

her into the mouth of the Neva. There he distributed gifts of money to the captain and crew and granted the ship permanent exemption from customs dues. With toasts and cannon salutes, she was renamed the *St. Petersburg*. Symbolically, at least, trade on the Baltic had begun.

During the winter of 1703–1704, work on the sea defenses of Kronstadt followed Peter's personally drawn plans. Huge sledlike boxes filled with stones were hauled out over the frozen surface of the gulf. Holes were chopped in the ice, and the boxes were lowered through them to serve as foundations for the new fort. But Peter did not stop there. All during the winter, he made preparations to clear the southern approaches of St. Petersburg in Livonia. Sheremetev was to storm Dorpat. He himself would lay siege to Narva.

With Menshikov, Peter arrived under the walls of Narva in June of 1704. Here, on the scene of his greatest humiliation, history threatened to repeat itself. As before, the siege artillery was late in coming up, and the troops could only dig in to repel the sorties of the Swedish garrison. As before, a strong Swedish relief force was reported on the march, and a Russian column was dispatched to intercept it. As before, Peter removed himself from the combat area and left the command to someone else; but here all parallels to the earlier campaign ended.

Seasoned Russian troops trounced the advancing Swedes, who retreated in confusion to Reval. Thanks to Peter's goading, the siege artillery arrived, and he personally supervised the positioning of the guns. Then he hurried off to Dorpat to give impetus and direction to Sheremetev's spirtless siege. By changing the angle of the attack, he was able to take Dorpat within ten days.

He returned to Narva with Sheremetev's artillery and promptly put it to good use. General Ogilvie, a veteran of forty years in the Austrian army, reported "that he never saw any nation go better to work with their cannon and mortar than the Russians at Narva." When he had opened a breach in the walls, Peter offered Horn, the Swedish commander, generous terms of surrender, but he refused. Peter gave the command to attack, and within an hour the Russians were inside the city. There they went mad, butchering soldiers and civilians alike. Peter had all he could do to call off his war dogs. He dealt one of his men such a blow with his sword that he was nearly decapitated.

Unlike Charles, Peter took no pleasure in bloodshed. Once when a Saxon garrison had faced virtual annihilation rather than surrender, Charles had rewarded its commander with a gift of 5,000 ducats, as if the affair had been some sort of chivalrous game. Now Peter berated Horn because his stubborn defiance had caused so much senseless slaughter. Peter's wars were terribly destructive, but he never regarded war as an end in itself. It was only the means to an end, and the end was the creation of a new Russia as embodied in his new city of St. Petersburg.

Chapter 23

THE TSAR TAKES A WIFE

By degrees, Alexander Menshikov had filled the vacuum left in Peter's life by the death of Lefort. As a boy, he had been a pie vendor in the Moscow market, and he never learned to write beyond scrawling his name, but, like Lefort, he had a quick mind, a ready wit, and a gay heart. He had been an early recruit in Peter's play regiments, and he had accompanied the Great Embassy to Holland and England, where he had excelled everyone but the Tsar at shipbuilding. More recently, he had shown himself a daring and able commander in the field, and Peter had appointed him Governor General of St. Petersburg. In short, Menshikov was already high in the Tsar's favor when he rewarded his royal master by bringing him together with the woman who became the love of his life.

Catherine Skavronsky fell into Russian hands as a sort of prize of war at the siege of Marienburg in 1702. General Sheremetev was in his headquarters when a family of refugees was brought before him. It was headed by a

Lutheran pastor, Ernst Gluck, who carried a Slavonic Bible and asked to serve the Tsar as a translator. As Sheremetev listened, his eye was caught by a strikingly handsome girl among the Pastor's children. She had dark hair and eyes, a well-developed figure, and an uncommonly cheerful expression.

In response to Sheremetev's question Gluck explained that she was not his child, but the daughter of Livonian peasants, orphaned when she was three. He had taken her into his household, where she had learned to do chores and look after the other children. Sheremetev granted Gluck permission to go to Moscow, but he kept the pretty Livonian peasant for himself. Somehow or other, she later came under the protection of Menshikov. In the following summer, she was living in his Moscow villa along with his fiancée, Daria Arsenev, her younger sister, and her maiden aunt who served as chaperone. There, in the fall of 1703, Menshikov introduced Catherine to the Tsar. Peter was thirty-one. She was just nineteen.

Peter took an immediate liking to the girl. He had been quarreling with Anna Mons, and Catherine suited him. Unlike Anna, who demanded material rewards for her favors, Catherine gave herself generously. She had the abundant health and vitality to match his own, and her unfailing good humor was an antidote to his occasional fits of depression. A foreigner, she accepted the Russian people as her own, and she entered into his ambitions for a new Russia far more sympathetically than Eudoxia ever had. He fell deeply in love with her.

Since Menshikov felt the same way about Daria Arsenev, the Tsar and his favorite were drawn closer than ever. After the capture of Narva, they sent for the young ladies. For the sake of appearances, Daria's aunt and sister came along, but "Auntie," as Peter called her, cannot have been a very strict chaperone: Catherine was already pregnant when she arrived.

In Moscow that winter, she gave birth to their first child, a boy named for his father. In March, 1705, the Tsar was writing instructions for the care of "my little Petrushka." Pregnant again that summer, Catherine took the long journey with Daria to spend a month with Peter and Menshikov in Poland. She returned to Moscow to give birth to a second son, Paul.

Peter longed to marry Catherine, but he hesitated as long as Eudoxia was still alive in the convent. His letters to Menshikov hint darkly at his desire that her death would free him to remarry. Chaperonage was becoming a problem. As long as Peter and Menshikov were together, all was well, but when they were forced to separate, "Auntie" could not be with them both. She and the girls had to stay with one or the other. At Peter's urging, Menshikov married Daria in the summer of 1706, freeing her of the need of a chaperone. "Auntie" could now accompany Catherine and the Tsar.

Even so, Peter and Catherine were often apart, and he who had never written a line to Eudoxia wrote frequently to Catherine. His letters were joking, affectionate, and even tender. They were accompanied by gifts of figs, apples, oranges, lemons, or oysters, of which she was especially fond. At other times, he presented her with jewels, lace, or some such novelty as a Dresden clock under glass. Once he sent her an eight-foot giant from Calais, whom he described as "a French dwarf I have engaged."

He showed the same sort of tenderness and concern for

his new "city." For years, St. Petersburg was little more than a collection of log cabins, but from the first, Peter pictured a shining capital rising from the islands in the estuary. And why not? Amsterdam had been constructed on just such a salt marsh, and the brick and stone magnificence of London had risen from the ashes of the Great Fire in only thirty years. He commissioned Domenico Trezzini, an Italian architect, to be his Christopher Wren.

Since childhood, Peter had had no real home. The demands of war, politics, and his own inner restlessness kept him continually on the move, and he could seldom endure being in one place for more than a few months. Now, for the first time, St. Petersburg gave him the sense of a home he had been missing, and during his intervals there, he displayed a passionate domesticity. As early as 1704, he ordered flowering shrubs to adorn the muddy streets. He was so delighted by the arrival of a shipment of peonies that he sent for pansies and mint to provide color and scent for his "northern Eden."

He was blind to its defects. Even serious inconveniences struck him as only amusing eccentricities that enhanced the charm and interest of the place. The day after his arrival from Menshikov's wedding, the Neva overflowed its banks and flooded the floor of his "palace" to a depth of two feet, but he wrote to his favorite in a jovial mood, dating his letter from "Sank" Petersburg. "It was entertaining to watch the people . . . sit on the roofs and trees just as in the time of the Deluge."

In 1707, Peter and Catherine were deeply saddened by the deaths of their two young sons. They were to lose ten of their twelve children, but there was special pathos in the awareness that Petrushka and little Paul had never had a legal father. Perhaps for this reason, Peter overcame his scruples about remarrying while Eudoxia was still alive. In November, he and Catherine were formally wed in St. Petersburg.

Instead of holding the kind of public celebration he so enjoyed, Peter took care to keep the ceremony private. Despite recent Russian successes, the war was a tremendous drain, and the country was near the breaking point. To publicize the marriage of the Orthodox Tsar to a Livonian peasant who had been born a Catholic and raised a Lutheran might have further inflamed a rebellion that was already raging on the southern frontier.

Chapter 24

DESPOTISM AND REBELLION

Peter was an enlightened despot fifty years before enlightened despotism came into vogue. He was enlightened in that he attacked ignorance, superstition, corruption, and conservatism. He introduced scientific education, rational administration, and modern industry. He emancipated women, subsidized printing, and expanded commerce. A humanitarian desire to improve the life of his people motivated one reform after another.

Yet he was often ruthlessly despotic in the demands he made on these people. He aimed at progress, but the tool that lay ready to his hand for achieving it was the tsarist autocracy he had inherited from the past. That autocracy rested on serfdom, and the more ambitious his programs became, the heavier were the burdens on the serfs. In this sense, Peter's efforts to modernize Muscovy led not to freedom, but to slavery, not to progress, but to oppression.

The Northern War was a tremendous drain on manpower. From 1700 to 1709, more than 300,000 peasants were drafted into the army. The new mines, foundries, and factories required vast numbers of industrial serfs. Drafts of forced labor to work on Peter's expanding construction projects were even greater. Although the fortification of Azov and Taganrog began in 1696, it was still calling for 30,000 men a year ten years later. The repeated attempts to construct a Don-Volga canal consumed labor on the same scale. Workers in the Voronezh dockyards were regularly in short supply, and after the conquest of the Neva, Peter began building a fleet for the Baltic as well as for the Black Sea. The construction of St. Petersburg and Kronstadt was the most demanding of all.

Living and working conditions were appalling. Disease flourished in the Tsar's boomtowns. Malaria and other fevers lurked in the swamps of St. Petersburg. Its distance from the crop-producing regions made food scarce and expensive. Some historians have estimated that the building of the new capital cost half a million lives. Both soldiers and laborers escaped whenever they could. Nearly half of 15,000 dragoons stationed in Poland deserted. The number of Cossacks in the Ukraine and on the Don was swelled by thousands of fugitives from the army and labor forces.

To plug up this drain on his manpower, Peter tightened controls. Peasants were required to carry official identity cards or passports. Attempts to track down fugitives and deserters were intensified. When he disbanded the Streltsy, Peter turned over their police powers to the Preobrazhensky Guards, and the Office of the Preobrazhensky developed a secret section that was the first regularly organized secret police in Russia. Under Romodanovsky, it became an instrument of savage oppression.

The need for money produced a multitude of new taxes.

Kurbatov and his "profit makers" devised taxes on births and marriages, caps and boots, baths and lodging houses, firewood, stovepipes, and even drinking water. In the long run, these produced little income, but they created enormous ill will. To former state monopolies like alcohol and potash were added tobacco, playing cards, chessmen, and oak coffins. Worst of all was the monopoly on salt. In 1705, salt was priced so high that it was put beyond the reach of many poor peasants, who sickened and died without it.

Peter was not the first Tsar to levy burdensome taxes, require forced labor, or wage an unpopular war; but he was the first to do so on such a large scale, and the first to make his role so clearly visible. Earlier rulers had been screened from view by Byzantine tradition. Behind the high walls of the Kremlin, the Tsar was a remote and shadowy figure. The peasants had a saying, "God is high, and the Tsar is far off." Cruelty and injustice were considered the work, not of the Tsar, but of wicked boyars and ministers.

Peter broke through the Byzantine isolation of his predecessors. He strode about in full view of the people wearing German breeches and smoking a Dutch pipe. His face was not benignly masked in a patriarchal beard, but naked and terrible to see. Could such a one be the true Tsar?

Rumors ran riot. This one they called Peter was not the son of Alexis, but the child of a German woman, changed in the cradle for a baby girl who had been the actual first-born of Tsaritsa Natalia. Another tale had it that Peter was the bastard son of Franz Lefort, which explained why, in the triumphal parade after Azov, Lefort had ridden in a gold coach, while his son, the Tsar, marched behind on foot. Others said that the true Tsar had been done to death during the Great Embassy. He had been nailed up in a cask and thrown into the sea, and this fellow who smoked the devil's weed and shaved his boyars was a German impostor, the Antichrist, the Beast of the Apocalypse.

The wildest rumors circulated on the frontiers. Astrakhan was a haven for many Old Believers, exiled Streltsy, runaways, and malcontents ready to believe the worst. In July, 1705, it was rumored that the government planned to suspend all marriages for seven years, so that "Germans" in the Tsar's service could have their pick of Russian maidens. Fathers hastened to marry their daughters to good Russians before the ban could be put into effect. On August 10, there were a hundred weddings in a single day. During the feasting and drinking that followed, talk and feeling ran so high that it erupted into violence. A mob stormed government buildings and murdered officials. The next day, the rebels elected leaders and prepared for armed resistance.

The news reached Peter in Poland. He was seriously alarmed. He feared the violence would spread up the Volga like the revolt of Stenka Razin just before he was born. He ordered General Sheremetev with the main army to march all the way to Astrakhan. There he easily crushed the rebellion, but the main army was diverted from the campaign in Poland for more than a year. Meanwhile, the war took a turn for the worse.

In the summer of 1706, when everyone had expected that Charles would invade Russia, he advanced on Saxony instead. In panic, Augustus secretly sued for peace with Sweden. He withdrew from the Northern War. He renounced his claim to the throne of Poland and permitted a Swedish puppet to replace him as its king. Finally, he surrendered to Charles the Livonian noble, Baron Patkul, who had first inspired him with the idea of capturing Riga from

Sweden. The Treaty of Altranstädt, as it was called, was announced in November, 1706. Luckily for Peter, Charles did not begin to move toward the Russian frontier for another year. Unluckily, the Swedish advance to the east in 1707 coincided with a new rebellion in the Russian rear.

Fugitive peasants had been fleeing to the Cossacks in ever-increasing numbers. The Cossacks were supposed to return serfs to the authorities, but their sympathies were with the runaways, and they frequently allowed them to stay. During the Astrakhan uprising of 1705 and 1706, Peter had avoided pressing enforcement on the Cossacks for fear that they might join the rebels. In 1707, with order restored, he sent Prince Yury Dolgoruky to the Don with a military force to demand the return of fugitives and deserters. The Cossack Ataman (or chief) promised to cooperate, but a lesser chief named Bulavin surprised Dolgoruky in the night and massacred him and his force to the last man.

Bulavin called for wholesale rebellion. He announced that he would take Azov and Taganrog, free the forced laborers, and march on both Voronezh and Moscow. His example sparked separate uprisings farther east early in 1708. The Bashkirs raided and burned Russian settlements on the Kama and Ufa Rivers. The Tartars of Kazan followed suit on the Volga. There was restlessness and disorder stirring along the whole frontier when Bulavin, who had been recruiting reinforcements on the Dnieper River, returned to the attack on the Don.

In the spring of 1708, he captured Cherkassk, the capital of the Don Cossacks, and put their Ataman to death. Then he made the fatal mistake of dividing his army into three parts. Vasily Dolgoruky, the brother of the murdered Yury,

subdued the first of these early in July. When a second detachment was crushed on the march to Azov, Bulavin committed suicide. By the end of 1708, order was restored. But
the long-postponed Swedish invasion was well under way.
As he faced it, Peter was aware that there was an ever-
present danger of renewed rebellion at his rear.

Chapter 25

THE INVASION OF RUSSIA—
POLTAVA

In the late summer of 1707, Charles began to move eastward across Poland. His army of 45,000 men was the largest and best-equipped he had ever commanded. In January of 1708, he accelerated his leisurely advance and led a cavalry raid against Grodno with such lightning speed that he narrowly missed capturing Peter himself. The Tsar rode out of the town with Menshikov only two hours before its fall.

The Swedish army went into winter quarters near Minsk. In June, Charles resumed his march across the vast plains of Poland. He planned to advance on Moscow by way of Smolensk. En route, he would be reinforced by Lewenhaupt with troops and supplies from Riga. Meanwhile, General Leibecker was to sweep down from Finland, capture St. Petersburg, and reconquer the Baltic provinces.

The thirty-six-year-old Tsar was convalescing from one of the illnesses that attacked him with increasing frequency as he grew older. He could not take the field in person, but he sent orders to his commanders, Menshikov, Repnin, and

Sheremetev. They were to avoid pitched battles, to devastate the Polish countryside over which they retreated, and to harass the enemy flanks with cavalry raids. Their scorched-earth tactics and the mud of the spring thaw slowed Charles's advance, but he came steadily on.

On July 15, the young King had the first opportunity for the battle he had been seeking. On the opposite side of the little Bibich River, the Russian generals decided to risk a stand. Charles did not pause even long enough for his entire army to come up. He plunged into the river and waded across under heavy Russian fire in water that came up to his armpits. On the opposite bank, he launched a savage assault on Repnin's wing. Eventually it broke, and the Russian army withdrew.

Bibich was another in Charles's unbroken string of victories, but it gained him nothing. The main Russian army was still in good order. It still blocked the road to Smolensk, and it still outnumbered the Swedes, whose losses were harder to replace than those of the Russians. Charles decided to wait for Lewenhaupt with supplies and reinforcements, but early in August, his impatience got the better of him and he resumed his advance.

Thanks to Catherine's nursing, Peter was now well enough to join the army. It retreated slowly, destroying and burning. Russian cavalry, Cossacks, and Tartars harried the enemy flanks and rear. Columns of smoke rose from the burning Polish villages, and the fields were blackened stubble. The travel-weary Swedes were losing their ability to move with sudden bursts of speed.

In September, 1708, Charles reached the Russian frontier at last. Blackened fields and clouds of smoke on the horizon made it clear that the Tsar was willing to scorch

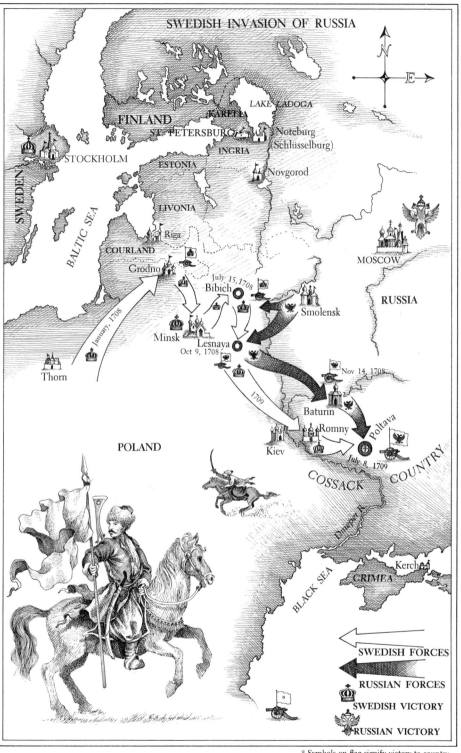

SWEDISH INVASION OF RUSSIA

N
E

FINLAND
LAKE LADOGA
KARELIA
ST. PETERSBURG
Noteburg
(Schlüsselburg)
STOCKHOLM
INGRIA
SWEDEN
ESTONIA
Novgorod
BALTIC SEA
LIVONIA
Riga
MOSCOW
COURLAND
Grodno
RUSSIA
July 15, 1708
Bibich
Smolensk
Minsk
Lesnaya
Oct 9, 1708
January, 1708
Nov 14, 1708
Thorn
1709
Baturin
POLAND
Romny
Poltava
Kiev
July 8, 1709
COSSACK COUNTRY
Kerch
CRIMEA
BLACK SEA

SWEDISH FORCES
RUSSIAN FORCES
SWEDISH VICTORY
RUSSIAN VICTORY

* Symbols on flag signify victory to country

his own as well as Polish earth. Peter expected that Charles would wait for Lewenhaupt with reinforcements, since these were now only four or five days' march away. When Charles suddenly broke camp and turned south into the Ukraine, the Tsar was puzzled. He sent Sheremetev and the main army after Charles. He himself stayed behind to intercept Lewenhaupt.

On October 9 at Lesnaya, Peter's army forced Lewenhaupt to give battle. The Swedes outnumbered the Russians 16,000 to 14,000, but they were crushed. Lewenhaupt managed to escape, but almost his entire force was killed or captured. Peter took all 16 Swedish cannon and 2,000 baggage wagons. He wrote, "This may be considered as our first victory, for we have never had a similar victory with regular troops and then with numbers inferior to those of the enemy." To add to his satisfaction, he heard from Apraxin that Leibecker's invasion had been repulsed. St. Petersburg and his beloved Catherine were safe.

Within a month, triumph gave way to consternation. The Tsar learned why Charles had turned south into the Ukraine. Mazepa, Ataman of the Ukranian Cossacks, had defected to the Swedes. If Mazepa gained the support of other Cossack leaders, he might swing over as many as 30,000 men. Worse, his example might well rekindle the rebellion that Peter's troops had barely stamped out on the Don and the Volga.

Decisive action was essential, and Peter struck hard. In joining Charles, Mazepa had left his capital city, Baturin, to a garrison. Peter dispatched Menshikov to attack and take it with all speed. Within a few days he succeeded. He put to death every last man, razed the walls and buildings, and set fire to the ruins. The speed and utter ruthlessness of the Tsar's justice brought the lesser Cossack chieftains to heel. They answered Peter's summons to an assembly, deposed Mazepa, and elected a new Ataman to replace him.

Charles went into winter quarters at Romny, but Peter enticed him out by feigning an advance that gave the fiery King hope of a pitched battle. While the Swedes were on the march, the most savage frost in memory struck Europe. There was ice on the canals as far south as Venice. The numbing cold on the windswept steppes was unimaginable. It was said that vodka froze in the cask, that spittle solidified before it hit the ground, that birds stiffened in flight and fell dead through the air. The Swedes suffered terrible losses. Some 3,000 died of exposure. Thousands more lost fingers, toes, hands, or feet.

Further action for that winter was out of the question, but in May, 1709, Charles resumed the offensive by attacking the little fortress of Poltava. It was an insignificant place, but Charles's shrunken forces were now too weak for effective siege operations. The action dragged on inconclusively for weeks and cost the besiegers more than the garrison. When Peter rejoined the main army on June 15, he sensed that final victory would soon be his. Taking personal command, he issued a stirring proclamation to his troops. "Either Russia will perish, or she will be reborn in a nobler shape. . . . Of Peter, it should be known that he does not value his own life, but only that Russia should live."

As the Russian army advanced to relieve Poltava, Charles rode out to reconnoiter. With his customary contempt for danger, he spurred his horse within musket range of a Russian outpost and was hit by a ball in the foot. The wound was not serious, but gangrene set in and was prevented from spreading only by cutting away the infected flesh. The twenty-seven-year-old King was weakened by fever and loss of blood, but running true to form, he attacked. He did not even use all the troops at his command. Leaving 5,000 men to guard Poltava, the baggage, and the bank of the river, he ordered 13,000 Swedes against three times that many Russians.

The attack began at dawn on July 8. Unable to walk, Charles had himself carried into the thick of the fighting on a litter. Of 24 bearers, 21 were killed. The Tsar also faced personal danger. One musket ball knocked off his hat. A second struck his saddle. A third bounced off the crucifix he wore around his neck. The Swedes fought as heroically as ever, but there were too many well-trained and well-armed Russians for them. By eleven in the morning, Charles had to order a retreat. His litter was smashed by a cannonball. Exhausted and clinging to the neck of a horse, he barely escaped capture.

More than 8,000 Swedes were taken prisoner, including a field marshal, four generals, and a number of senior officers. Charles, Mazepa, and about 1,000 men crossed the Dnieper River and took refuge in Turkey. They were all that was left of nearly 60,000 Swedes who had begun the campaign.

Peter was generous in victory. He invited the captured officers to a banquet on the battlefield and offered them a toast as "Our teachers in the art of war." To Apraxin he wrote, "Now, with the help of God, the final stone in the foundation of St. Petersburg has been laid." Best of all, he could tell Catherine, "In a word, the whole of the enemy's army is knocked on the head, and you will hear about it from us. Come here and congratulate us. Peter."

BOOK FOUR

Triumph and Tragedy

Chapter 26

THE INVASION OF EUROPE—
HANGÖ

Poltava was a turning point in Peter's reign. It so enhanced his prestige that he no longer had to fear armed uprisings at home. It gave him a breathing space to work on domestic reforms not directly related to the war. It removed Sweden from the ranks of the great powers and put Russia in her place. It ended the threat of western invasion for a century, and was followed instead by a Russian invasion of Europe.

This invasion was diplomatic, military, dynastic, and commercial, but the diplomatic developments were first to appear. As soon as Augustus heard the news of Poltava, he sent congratulations, protestations of undying friendship, and a request to meet the Tsar at Thorn in Poland. Peter agreed, and in October they signed a new treaty. Before they had finished their discussions the King of Denmark was proposing an alliance. Soon afterward, Peter concluded a third treaty with the King of Prussia.

These selfish and uncertain allies would prove of little

use, but Peter could not be sure that Charles was no longer a threat. If he should arouse the Sultan to the attack, Russian forces would be pinned down in the south, and Baltic allies would be helpful for the defense of St. Petersburg. Certainly, Peter was not fooled by Augustus's vows of permanent devotion. At their first meeting in 1698, the two monarchs had exchanged swords. In Thorn, Peter pointed out that, while he was still wearing the King's sword, Augustus was not wearing the Tsar's. Augustus earnestly assured Peter that he prized his sword, but because he had departed Dresden in great haste, it had somehow been left behind.

"Well, then." Peter smiled. "Let me give you another just like it." He then produced the original sword, which he had discovered with the captured baggage of Charles XII at Poltava.

In November, 1709, Peter joined General Sheremetev to begin the siege of Riga. He personally fired the first three shells of the opening bombardment and directed a vigorous military offensive against Sweden's other Baltic possessions. Elbing surrendered early in 1710. In June, Apraxin took Vyborg. Riga fell in July, Pernau and Arensburg in August, Kexholm and Reval in September.

Peter supplemented these conquests with the first of a whole series of dynastic marriages that linked the Romanovs with German royalty. The Duke of Courland asked for the hand of Peter's niece, the Tsarevna Anna, and the two were married in St. Petersburg in November, 1710. Following the sudden death of the Duke two months later, Peter sent Russian troops into Courland to add another link to his Baltic chain.

The transformation of the Baltic from a Swedish to a

Russian lake had far-reaching diplomatic and commercial consequences. It gained Russia control of resources of vital importance to the great maritime powers. In Peter's day, the naval stores of the Baltic were what the oil of the Middle East became in the twentieth century. The navies of the world were moved by wind, not oil, but to catch and hold that wind, they needed the great masts of Riga and the hemp of the Ukraine.

A ship of the line might remain in service for fifty or sixty years, but its masts and hempen rigging had to be regularly replaced. Lesser masts and spars came from many forests, but Riga had a virtual monopoly of the great masts required to support the sail of a ship of the line. They came from far in the interior of Poland. Trees were felled in the winter, hauled over the snow to stream banks, and assembled into rafts in the spring. They formed great floating islands of as many as a thousand trees. They carried whole families with their horses, cattle, and poultry on the long voyage down the Düna River.

At Riga, the masts were marked, or "bracked," as first, second, or third quality. Peter had often seen the bracking of the great masts of Riga at the king's yard in Deptford, and well understood their importance. The extent of English dependence on Russian masts and hemp is illustrated in a letter from the British Secretary of State. He wrote, "If the fleet of merchant ships now loading in the Baltic should by any accident miscarry, it would be impossible for His Majesty to fit out any ships of war for the next year, by which means the whole navy will be rendered perfectly useless."

The need for naval stores was a vital stimulus for expanding trade with Russia, and it was an important influence in international relations throughout the eighteenth century. It even played a part in the outcome of the American Revolution. Because a Russian Empress, Catherine the Great, favored the French over the English in 1780, there was a French fleet under DeGrasse off Yorktown, while the British fleet was kept in New York harbor because its masts were too rotten to trust to the open sea.

During the latter part of 1710, Peter had a welcome respite from campaigning and enjoyed life in St. Petersburg with Catherine. They had lost their two sons, Peter and Paul, three years before, and a girl named for Catherine had died the following year, but now they had two healthy daughters, Anna and Elizabeth. At twenty-six, Catherine was far from finished with childbearing, and they still hoped for a son. The pleasures of life in St. Petersburg were cut short by news that Charles XII, who was still in Turkey, had at last persuaded the Sultan to declare war. Early in 1711, Peter set out for Preobrazhensky to prepare for a new campaign.

Peter had worn down the Swedes by luring them deep into the interior of Russia. Now he reversed his strategy. He would strike first, invade the Turkish provinces of Bessarabia and Moldavia (now Rumania), and call on their Christian minorities to rise in revolt against their heathen masters. He was so confident of his success that he granted Catherine's request that she and her little court be allowed to accompany the army.

On July 8, 1711, the second anniversary of Poltava, they were already deep in enemy territory on the banks of the Pruth. Peter called a council of war and made the fateful decision to cross the river and march still farther south through the stifling heat and parched countryside. Ten days later, an advance detachment reported the alarming news that the Grand Vizier was advancing with an overwhelming force. Suddenly, fewer than 40,000 Russians were surrounded by nearly 200,000 Turks. In the first day's fighting the Russians resisted fiercely and inflicted heavy losses, but their situation was desperate.

Peter had made the same sort of mistakes that had lured Charles to his destruction. He had marched deep into enemy territory without adequate supplies. He had counted on the support of Christian minorities that did not materialize. He had overrated his own strength and seriously underestimated the strength of the Turks. Only a miracle could save him from defeat and the double humiliation of captivity for himself and his beloved Catherine.

But Peter did not make Charles's final mistake. He did not delude himself that he was invincible. Learning from some captured Turks that the Grand Vizier was empowered to negotiate peace, he sent word that he was willing to discuss terms.

As luck would have it, the Grand Vizier was anxious to save his army for a campaign in the Balkans. He was unaware of Peter's weakness and acutely conscious of his own losses. His elite corps had suffered so heavily that it was on the point of mutiny. The terms he proposed were relatively mild. Russia must return Azov and Taganrog, withdraw the permanent embassy in Constantinople, and grant Charles XII freedom of passage to Sweden. Peter consented, and the agreement was signed on July 23, 1711.

His losses on the Sea of Azov meant that Peter would have to postpone his ambitions on the Black Sea indefinitely, but he had been prepared to sacrifice much more. As it was, his Baltic conquests were intact, and his army was saved from certain destruction. With his cheerful and uncomplaining Catherine beside him, he headed north.

He was now in his fortieth year, and the campaign had affected his health. Instead of returning to St. Petersburg, he took his doctor's advice to go to Karlsbad for the waters. There he completed the arrangements for the marriage of his son, Tsarevich Alexis, to Princess Charlotte von Wolfenbüttel. Since she was the sister-in-law of the Austrian Emperor, the alliance joined the Romanovs to one of the most illustrious royal families in Europe. His success at Poltava had given Peter the necessary prestige to make such a match. Alexis and Charlotte were wed in Torgau, Poland, in October, 1711. For the first time in two centuries, a Tsarevich married a foreigner. All later Romanov princes would also marry foreigners, most of them Germans.

At Torgau, Peter met the famous German philosopher and mathematician Gottfried Wilhelm Leibniz. He warmed to the German's enthusiasm for Russia's future and his proposals for the reform of education and the establishment of an academy of science. For his part, Leibniz was fascinated by the Tsar. He wrote, "I can never cease marveling at the liveliness and intelligence of this great sovereign. He gathers about him on all sides learned men, and when he talks with them, they are absolutely astonished at the knowledge he shows of their business. . . . I hope we shall learn through his aid whether Asia is joined to North America."

Returning to St. Petersburg, Peter was delighted to be reunited with Catherine. From Karlsbad, he had written her, "You write that, on account of the cure, I should not hurry to you. It is quite evident that you have found somebody better than me. Kindly write about it. Is it one of ours or a man of Thorn?" But although he frequently used this joking tone with her, he was in dead seriousness about his desire to have her receive the public honor due her as his wife. In March, 1712, he arranged an elaborate public celebration of their private wedding of five years before. Then, there had been opposition to his union with a Livonian peasant. Now, Catherine had won the heart of the army by her courage and steadfastness during the Turkish campaign, and even the most conservative boyars welcomed her softening influence on Peter's savage temper.

During this period and for some time after, Peter sought Danish naval support for a Russian landing on the coast of Sweden. Since he already commanded a considerable fleet of his own, some observers have been puzzled by his reluctance to attack Sweden without allies. The reason is seen in the comments of an English admiral, Sir John Norris, who inspected Russian ships of the line in Reval. He described them as "in every way equal to the best of that rank in our country and more handsomely finished. The Tsar's only want is to make seamen out of his soldiers."

Making seamen out of soldiers was no easy feat. Sailing was new to Russia. The fleet was frozen in port for more than half the year. There was no merchant marine to train seamen who could then be pressed into the Tsar's navy. The Baltic abounded in rocky islands and sheer headlands that cut off wind and made sailing difficult for even the most experienced seamen. Peter's ships were more than a match for Charles's, but until he had the crews that could sail them properly, it would be suicide to entrust a landing expedition to their care.

A galley fleet was one solution to this problem. Galleys did not depend on wind, and although Russians were new to the salt sea, their rivers had taught them to use oars.

When Peter launched an amphibious invasion of Finland in 1713, he used 93 galleys, and the campaign was a great success.

In 1714, Peter put to sea with 20 ships of the line and 200 galleys. In August, they encountered an inferior Swedish force off Hangö. The enemy ships of the line fled, but a number of smaller vessels took refuge in a fiord. Peter followed them in and captured a frigate, nine galleys, and the control of the Åland Islands.

The Tsar rated the victory at Hangö on a level with Poltava. This was an exaggeration, but on his triumphant voyage back to St. Petersburg, he could take satisfaction in the achievements of the past five years. He had cleared his land of invaders, and his troops had carried the war to foreign soil. His territory ringed a great part of the Baltic, and his fleet had tested its mettle against the Swedes. Final victory was only a matter of time. Yet even when prospects were at their brightest, Peter was reminded of a danger that threatened his life work from another quarter.

Chapter 27

THE SHADOW ON THE THRONE

Peter often held shipboard banquets in his new harbor at Kronstadt, and at one of them, a young naval officer named Mishukov suddenly burst into tears. Peter asked him what was the matter.

"It's like this," the young man began, then hesitated. He had drunk much wine. "This place, the new capital, the Baltic fleet, all the Russian sailors, and finally myself, Lieutenant Mishukov, commander of a frigate, all know how much we owe to your favor, and realize that this is all your work. And as I was thinking about this just now, I realized that you are not getting any younger, and so I burst into tears." After a pause, he added gloomily, "And who is there to take your place?"

"What do you mean?" Peter demanded. "I've got a Tsarevich, an heir."

"Oh, yes." Mishukov shrugged. "But he's an idiot and will undo all your work."

Peter fetched the young lieutenant a blow on the head.

"You are a fool," he growled. "You cannot say such things in public."

Yet it is certain that Peter himself thought them in private, and the fear that Alexis might one day undo what he had created worked like a poison in his system.

The only child of a loveless marriage, the sickly and timid Alexis was by temperament the exact opposite of his father. His greatest pleasure was in reading religious books. He had a taste for scholarship and did well in his studies, but was frightened by his father's spasmodic efforts to interest him in military or naval matters. When he was twelve, the Tsar took him to Archangel for the summer, and the following year, to the storming of Nyenskantz. Afterward, Alexis was allowed to withdraw into his books, but when he was fifteen, Peter sent his tutor on a long diplomatic mission abroad and never got around to providing another. Left without supervision, Alexis turned from the pleasures of books to those of the bottle.

As heir to the throne, he became the center of a circle of churchmen and conservatives who opposed Peter's reforms. His mother's relatives persuaded him to visit her in secret. When he admitted to his confessor that he had sinned by wishing for the death of his father, the priest replied, "God will forgive you. We all wish his death, for the burden on the people is great."

Alexis's terror of the Tsar is illustrated by two incidents in his young manhood. At twenty, when he was sent to study in Saxony, he was haunted by the fear that he would die abroad without a priest to administer the last rites. He wrote his confessor to send him one, but the letter shows him as frightened of his father on earth as of his Father in Heaven: "Tell him to come to me in great secrecy, to lay aside all marks of his condition, to shave his beard and hair, and to wear a wig and German clothes."

Following his marriage to Princess Charlotte in 1711, Alexis remained abroad on military assignments for two years. When he returned to St. Petersburg in 1713, Peter asked to see his sketches of military fortifications. Alexis was twenty-three, but he was thrown into such a panic at the thought of his father asking him to demonstrate his sketching ability that he tried to shoot himself in the hand. He bungled and missed, but he suffered severe powder burns.

In St. Petersburg, he sank into indolent drunkenness. He either abused his sweet young wife or neglected her. When she was eight months pregnant, he abandoned her with only an hour's notice to go to Karlsbad. During the six months he was gone, he did not write even to acknowledge the birth of their daughter. On his return, he openly took as his mistress a Finnish serf girl, Efrosinia.

In October, 1715, Charlotte gave birth to a second child. This time, it was a boy named Peter. She bloomed briefly with the pride of having produced an heir to the throne, but relapsed into illness and died soon after. Guilt-stricken, Alexis swooned three times at her bedside. When he returned from the funeral, he was brought an envelope addressed ominously in his father's hand, *A Message to My Son*.

Peter pronounced Alexis "unfit for the handling of state affairs." He deplored his "bad stubborn character" and unwittingly showed his unfitness as a father in a revealing sentence: "How much have I not only scolded, but beaten you for this, and think of how many years I have not spoken to you!" In conclusion, he threatened Alexis that, unless he changed his ways, "I will cut you off wholly from the succession, like a gangrenous growth."

On November 10, before Alexis could answer his father's letter, Catherine gave birth to her eighth child. It was a boy. For the first time since the deaths of little Peter and Paul in 1707, Alexis was not the sole Tsarevich.

The Tsar was overjoyed. Mourning for the dead Charlotte was suspended for three days to celebrate the birth of little Peter, as he was christened. The Tsar wrote to an officer of the Guards, "I announce to you that this night God has given me a recruit named after his father. God grant me to see him under a musket. I beg you to announce it with my compliments to the officers and soldiers. What is spent for drink, write down to my account."

The superstitious Alexis saw the birth of a rival as an omen. After consulting with his secret advisers, Alexander Kikin and Vasily Dolgoruky, he renounced his claims to the throne in a groveling and abject letter.

Peter's reply was delayed by another serious attack of illness. He came so close to death that church dignitaries were called to administer the last rites, but then he rallied. When he was strong enough to answer Alexis's letter, he rejected his renunciation of the throne as inadequate. "Either change your nature . . . or become a monk." Alexis promptly answered that he would become a monk, but Peter was still not satisfied.

Peter's position seems highly unreasonable. He bullied Alexis and despised him for being bullied. He demanded his submission and condemned his submissiveness. He forced him to choose and rejected his choice.

Yet both Peter and Alexis knew that the choice had not been sincere. Alexis might enter a monastery, but as Kikin had said to him, "To put on a cowl does not fasten it to your head with a nail. You can take it off again." He could renounce his claim to the throne every day of Peter's life and revive it again at the moment of his death. Their situation was hopeless, and hopelessness was something that an optimist like Peter could not accept. Faced with an insoluble dilemma, he lost his characteristic decisiveness and refused to decide. When Alexis repeated to his face his offer to become a monk, the Tsar put him off. "Think it over carefully," he said. "I will give you six months. Then you can write me again."

With this farewell, Peter set off with Catherine for an extended sojourn in the west. In April, they were in Danzig for the marriage of Peter's niece, Catherine Ivanovna, to the Duke of Mecklenburg. In May, he conferred with Frederick IV of Denmark in Altona. In June, while taking the waters in Pyrmont, he discussed educational reforms with Liebniz and building plans for his capital with the young French architect, Leblond.

In July, he sailed a Russian fleet from Rostock to Copenhagen, where he hoped to enlist naval support for a landing on the Swedish coast. When secret British opposition frustrated this plan, the Tsar tried to forget his frustration by sailing with a huge convoy in the Baltic. Its 700 merchant vessels were escorted by 80 Dutch, Danish, English, and Russian men-of-war. He detached a squadron from this international armada to reconnoiter the Swedish coast, but ventured too close. Swedish shore batteries scored a hit on his flagship and seriously damaged another vessel. Now that Charles XII was back on native soil, any invasion attempt could count on stout resistance.

Back in Copenhagen, Peter decided to postpone his proposed landing until the following year. He would winter in Amsterdam and negotiate with George I of England for the support of the British fleet. Since Catherine was again pregnant, he would go ahead, leaving her to follow at a slower pace. Before he left, he wrote to Alexis in St. Petersburg. "You have had enough time for reflection," he said. "On receiving this letter, make your decision at once."

The next courier brought word that the Tsarevich was on his way to join his father. Apparently, instead of becoming a monk, Alexis had determined to "change his nature." But in Danzig, the reports of his progress suddenly ceased. Alexis had vanished into thin air. The news reached Peter in Amsterdam, where he had once again fallen seriously ill. From his sickbed, he dispatched secret instructions to Weide in Danzig to begin a search. But before his spies had reported any definite word, Peter embarked on a new diplomatic venture.

Chapter 28

PETER IN PARIS

The year 1717 began gloomily. Peter was racked with illness, troubled about Alexis, and lonely for Catherine. He was temporarily cheered to hear from her that "The Lord God has given us another recruit,"—that is, that she had borne another son on January 14. But the baby died the next day and, as he wrote her, "changed joy to grief." He wanted to speed to her side to comfort her, but he was forty-four and lacked the recuperative power of his youth. He suffered a relapse that made travel impossible. Catherine recovered first and came to Amsterdam to nurse him back to health.

Having finally accepted that naval support from England was out of the question, Peter decided to seek friendship with France. In her long rivalry with the Austrian Empire, France had traditionally allied herself with Sweden, Poland, and Turkey on the Austrian flanks. Since the traditional French allies were also traditional Russian enemies, Peter had, until now, viewed France as a threat, but the balance of power was shifting. Louis XIV was dead, and since England and Holland had withheld support, it was only reasonable for Peter to explore what France might do.

Peter began negotiations through the embassy at The Hague, but on March 20, he informed the French ambassador that he would take personal charge and journey to Paris for the purpose. He left the very next day.

It was twenty years since the Great Embassy had set off for the west. Now, as then, the Tsar preserved the fiction of an incognito, but he was no longer the unknown ruler of a remote Asiatic country. He was the celebrated monarch of a great European power. His retainers were not the ignorant novices of the Great Embassy. Men like Tolstoy, Shafirov, and Kurakin were widely traveled and accomplished diplomats. Peter's curiosity was as insatiable as ever. His wide-ranging interests prompted frequent detours and delays to inspect factories, fortresses, and novelties of any kind, and he was constantly on the lookout for skilled foreigners to recruit into his service.

He left Catherine in Holland. She was once again pregnant, and he was not certain that she would be received at the French court with proper respect. With sixty retainers and servants, he crossed Belgium through Antwerp, Brussels, Bruges, and Ostend. At Dunkerque, he was welcomed by the head of a French delegation, De Liboy. On the journey to Paris, De Liboy found the Tsar "rather exacting and irascible." Apparently, Peter's uncertainty about Alexis was making him more irritable than usual.

On his arrival in Paris on May 5, the Tsar behaved boorishly. He refused the luxurious living quarters assigned to him in the Louvre. At the state dinner for sixty guests, he asked for bread and radishes, sampled six kinds of wine, drank two glasses of beer, and drove off to the simpler apartments arranged for him at the Hotel Lesdiguières. There he had his camp bed set up in the smallest of the dressing rooms and went to sleep.

After this unorthodox beginning, Peter was on his good behavior. He received the Regent, the Duke of Orleans, and later the youthful King Louis XV. Peter wrote Catherine that the King was "only a finger or two bigger than our Luke [his favorite dwarf], very handsome in his face and build, and very intelligent for his age, which is seven." The giant Tsar and the child King sat in armchairs conversing through interpreters for a quarter of an hour. Then Peter picked up the boy, kissed him several times, and led him out to his carriage by the hand. He showed the same fatherly informality on his return visit to the Tuileries. As little Louis was coming to meet him, Peter swung him up in his arms and ran up the steps to the palace. He had thoughts of a match between Louis and his eight-year-old Elizabeth and wanted to make a good impression.

Villeroi wrote to Madame De Maintenon, widow of Louis XIV, "This Prince, said to be barbarous, is not so at all; he has displayed to us sentiments of grandeur, of generosity, and of politeness that we by no means expected." The mother of the Duke of Orleans wrote, "I received today a great visit, that of my hero, the Tsar. I find that he has very good manners. . . . He is polite toward everyone and is much liked."

Peter had a particular interest in the architecture of Paris and of the palaces and gardens of Versailles, Fontainebleau, and St. Cloud. He was seeking ideas that could be applied to the beautification of St. Petersburg, and he was delighted with the gift of several leather-bound volumes of engravings of the gardens and palaces of Versailles.

He inspected the military hospital of the Invalides. He discussed fortifications at the Louvre and coinage at the Mint, where a medal bearing his likeness was struck while he looked on. He toured the botanical gardens and the University of the Sorbonne, observed a surgical operation for cataracts, and paid several visits to the Gobelin tapestry works, which he hoped to imitate in Russia.

The distinguished courtier Saint-Simon was struck by the liveliness of his curiosity. "It embraced everything, disdained nothing in the smallest detail useful. It was marked and enlightened, esteeming only what merited to be esteemed, and exhibited in a clear light the intelligence, justice, and ready appreciation of his mind. Everything showed in the Tsar the vast extent of his knowledge and a sort of logical harmony of ideas." As a result of his visit to the French Academy of Sciences, Peter was elected an extraordinary member.

French observers were astonished by what he ate and drank at his two regular meals. Saint-Simon declared it inconceivable. De Liboy wrote, "The Tsar has a head cook who prepares two or three dishes for him every day, and who uses for this purpose enough wine and meat to serve a table of eight. . . . He likes sharp sauces, brown and hard bread, and green peas. He eats many sweet oranges and apples and pears."

Saint-Simon thought the Tsar very handsome except for "the twitching of the face, not often occurring, but which appeared to distort his eyes and all his physiognomy and was frightful to see. It lasted a moment, gave him a wild and terrible air, and passed away as quickly." He had a disturbing habit of leaping into any coach "which he could lay his hands on." Once, he commandeered the carriage of a French noblewoman "who had come to gape at him" and drove off to Boulogne with it. "The owner was much astonished to find she must journey back on foot."

Despite his idiosyncrasies, Peter's visit to Paris was a brilliant personal success. He recruited more than a hundred French artisans and technicians into his service. But just as with the Great Embassy, he failed in his diplomatic designs. Because England and Holland brought pressure on France to resist his proposals, he achieved only a treaty of friendship and good will. It improved Peter's overall position, but gained no immediate aid in ending the Northern War.

He left Paris on June 30. Because his health was bothering him, he did not rejoin Catherine in Holland, but went instead to Spa to take the waters. Here at last he turned his full attention to the problem of Alexis.

Chapter **29**

THE TRAGEDY OF ALEXIS

When Alexis left St. Petersburg with his mistress, Efrosinia, toward the close of 1716, he had no intention of going to his father. Peter's frequent illnesses had persuaded him that the Tsar could not live much longer. If he could hide out abroad for a year or two, his father's death would free him to return to Russia. His friend Kikin recommended Vienna as his best hope of asylum. Thanks to his marriage to Princess Charlotte, Alexis was the brother-in-law of the Emperor Charles VI, who was therefore obliged to grant him protection. In Danzig, he disguised Efrosinia as a page and himself as a Russian officer. Under an assumed name, he then made all haste for Vienna.

Late on the evening of November 21 in the Austrian capital, the Imperial Vice-Chancellor was prevented from retiring by the arrival of a mysterious foreign visitor. Alexis burst in upon him and poured out his woes in such a torrent of words and tears that the minister could scarcely understand him. The Tsarevich insisted he was in fear of his life and implored the Emperor's protection. The Emperor called a hasty and highly secret council, then agreed to offer Alexis asylum on one condition: he must consent to shut himself up in the mountain fortress of Ehrenburg, high in the snows of the Tirolean Alps. Alexis eagerly agreed.

The Tsarevich was spirited away to the Tirol with the utmost secrecy. At Ehrenburg, security was so tight that his true identity was unknown even to the commander. Strangers were to be kept away from the gates, and the mysterious prisoner was to receive no letters or communications except from the Imperial Chancery. Alexis did not chafe at this confinement. He had his books, his little page, and a generous allowance for food and drink. He began to breathe more easily.

Meanwhile, Peter had guessed the direction of his son's flight and had instructed his Austrian ambassador to search him out. In March, the ambassador heard rumors of a curious prisoner in a Tirolean fortress. He dispatched Rumyantsov, a giant Guards officer, to investigate. As soon as Rumyantsov had identified Alexis, the ambassador delivered a letter Peter had given him for the Emperor. It requested the immediate return of the Tsarevich under armed escort. The Emperor pretended to know nothing of the matter, but he took the letter and promised to investigate. Then he dispatched a copy of the Tsar's letter to Alexis.

On learning that his hiding place had been discovered, the Tsarevich became hysterical. He was inconsolable until he was told that he might move to a still more distant fortress outside Naples. With his little page, he set off the next day. The Austrian secretary who accompanied them reported that, except for "fits of frequent and excessive drunkenness," the trip went well. He did not know that Rumyantsov and his bloodhounds had been tracking them the entire way.

In July in Spa, Peter laid plans to recover his runaway son. He chose as his special emissary Count Peter Tolstoy, a skilled diplomat who was fluent in Italian. At the Russian Count's hint that the Tsar would use force if necessary, Charles granted Tolstoy and Rumyantsov permission to interview the Tsarevich in Naples. However, he insisted that Alexis could not be forcibly removed from his protection; he must go of his own free will.

It was October when the unsuspecting Alexis was suddenly confronted by the old Count and the giant Guards officer in Naples. Thinking they meant to kill him, he was nearly unhinged, but Tolstoy suddenly became all charm. He assured Alexis that his father meant to pardon him and delivered a letter from Peter to that effect. It required five interviews to win the Tsarevich around. Tolstoy coaxed, reasoned, wheedled, and threatened. In the end, Efrosinia proved to be the key. Four months pregnant, her identity had been discovered at last, and the suggestion that she might be taken from him was too much for Alexis. He was an idler, a coward, and a drunkard, but he genuinely loved Efrosinia. He agreed to return to Russia, provided he could marry her first. Peter consented to the marriage, but insisted that it take place on Russian soil. Prince Vasily Dolgoruky saw through the ruse and wrote to a friend, "Have you heard that the fool of a Tsarevich is coming back because his father has promised he can marry Efrosinia? He'll have a grave, not a wedding."

It was a long trip home. Alexis left his pregnant mistress

in Venice so that he could travel ahead at a faster pace. Finally, on February 14, 1718, sixteen months after it had begun, the odyssey that had led him halfway across Europe ended in the Great Hall of the Kremlin in Moscow.

Peter had chosen this ancient setting deliberately. With his flair for the dramatic, he sensed that this was the moment to emphasize the antiquity and majesty of the Tsar's role. All the great magnates of church and state were assembled. When Peter had seated himself on the throne, Alexis was brought in. He wore no sword, to indicate that he was a prisoner, and he immediately threw himself at his father's feet.

Peter raised him up and ordered the reading of Alexis's signed confession. When it was finished, the Tsar spoke. He dwelt solemnly on his son's crimes, but since Alexis had confessed and renounced his claims to the throne, he, the Tsar, was prepared to pardon him on condition that he reveal the names of all those who had been his accomplices. He then ordered read a manifesto which, after enumerating Alexis's offenses for a third time, declared the little Tsarevich Peter Petrovich the rightful heir to the throne. The entire assembly then repaired to the Cathedral of the Assumption, where Alexis swore on a Bible his allegiance to his little half brother.

Alexis's advisers, Kikin and Vasily Dolgoruky, were arrested and brought to Moscow in chains. Kikin was put to death. In recognition of his services in putting down the rebel Bulavin, Dolgoruky escaped with exile. Others were questioned, and the investigation extended to Eudoxia. It was discovered that, inside the nunnery, she had been leading the life of a worldly aristocrat. She had even taken a lover. The lover, Alexis's confessor, his servant, the Bishop of Rostov, and a number of others were put to death. Many more were exiled, beaten, or disgraced, but when the Tsar returned to St. Petersburg in March, Dolgoruky's dire prediction that Alexis would have a grave instead of a wedding was not fulfilled. He accompanied his father.

In St. Petersburg, the Tsarevich was given his freedom in a house next door to Catherine's palace. He still hoped for a wedding, but he was not informed when Efrosinia arrived in St. Petersburg. She was secreted in the Fortress of Saints Peter and Paul, where she gave birth to a child. What became of it—or even what its sex was—is shrouded in mystery.

Late in May, Alexis was called to the summer palace of Peterhof. There he found Efrosinia with his father. The reunion for which he had yearned in his dreams proved a nightmare. As he listened in horror, Efrosinia recited in detail all he had said against his father, how he had longed for his overthrow, how he had planned to rule when he became Tsar, how he would leave St. Petersburg, its ships, and its harbor to rot. He would do just as Mishukov had prophesied at the banquet in Kronstadt.

Efrosinia was not tortured. It is not known why she turned against Alexis. Perhaps she was frightened. She may have been bribed. In any case, she sealed his doom. If St. Petersburg were to be saved, Alexis must be excluded from the succession, and this could be guaranteed only by his death.

Peter knew this in his heart, but he evaded the truth. He also evaded the responsibility for condemning his own son. He appointed a court of 128 of the great magnates of the realm to try him. On June 28, it met. The Tsarevich was twice questioned under the lash. On July 5, he was convicted of having plotted against the Tsar. By unanimous vote, he was sentenced to death.

Peter neither confirmed nor executed the sentence. Two days later, Alexis died under mysterious circumstances. Various accounts reported that he had died of a stroke, that he had been smothered, that he had been poisoned, and that he had been bled to death. The Austrian ambassador wrote that Peter himself had beheaded his son. It is unlikely that any of the more lurid reports are true. The effects of fear, torture, and failing health are sufficient to explain the death of Alexis, but this can hardly excuse Peter's guilt. However Alexis died, Peter was as responsible for his death as if he had murdered him with his own hands.

Chapter **30**

VICTORY AND BACKWARDNESS

In May, 1718, six weeks before the death of Alexis, Peter opened peace discussions with Sweden on one of the Åland Islands. In time, the negotiations became entangled in a complex diplomatic web that reached into the courts of nearly all Europe. They were punctuated by the death of Charles XII at the siege of a Norwegian fortress in December, 1718, and by Russian raids on the Swedish coast during the next three summers. They were broken off in the fall of 1719 and resumed at Nystadt in the spring of 1721. They were concluded late that summer.

Peter was sailing on the Gulf of Finland in September when he got the news. He gave the people of St. Petersburg their first inkling by sailing his yacht into the mouth of the Neva, firing repeated salutes from his brass cannon. The excited crowds that flocked to the bank of the river knew it could mean only one thing. Peace. Peace with victory.

The clanging of church bells spread across the city. The cannon of the Fortress of Saints Peter and Paul added their deep-throated thunder. From the Admiralty wharf, the smiling Tsar and Tsaritsa led a joyful procession to the Church of the Holy Trinity for a service of thanksgiving. By the time they emerged, barrels of wine, mead, and beer were being set up in the streets. The Tsar gave the first toast. Merrymaking and dancing in the streets continued for several days.

The Treaty of Nystadt gave Russia not simply a window on the west, but the entire coast from Vyborg in Finland to Riga in Livonia. In return, Russia gave Sweden a money compensation, the right to buy grain duty-free in certain ports, and a promise not to meddle in Sweden's internal affairs. After Poltava, Peter had toasted the enemy as Russia's teachers in the art of war. After Nystadt, he wrote his ambassador in Paris with a similar reference to education.

"All students of science normally finish their course in seven years. Our schooling has lasted three times as long, but, praise God, it has all ended so well that it could not be better."

At first, Peter had studied western models only for the art of war, but Sweden illustrated the military advantages of efficient civil administration. During the nine years from Narva to Poltava, Charles had not so much as set foot on home soil, and yet his government continued to function smoothly. In Russia, nothing ran smoothly unless it had the Tsar's personal attention. As Pososhkov put it, "The great monarch works hard and accomplishes nothing. There are few to help him. The Tsar pulls uphill alone with the strength of ten, but millions pull downhill."

After Poltava, Peter tried to rectify this failing. Decrees flowed from his pen at the rate of one every three days.

Later even this furious pace was doubled. Individually, these decrees dealt with specific and practical problems, but taken as a whole they reveal an attempt to create a state "governed with rule and precept, not custom and caprice." Peter borrowed his political models from the west, but he adapted them to native traditions. He erected the structure of a modern European state on the foundations of a primitive Muscovite past.

In Sweden, Denmark, and Prussia, government departments were run by boards known as colleges. Leibniz wrote Peter, "There cannot be good administration except with colleges: Their mechanism is like that of watches, whose wheels mutually keep each other in motion." The comparison was appealing to an amateur watch repairman like Peter, and he used colleges widely in remodeling his administration.

Before he had invaded Turkey in 1711, he had appointed a Senate of nine members to act as a sort of collective Tsar in his absence, and it continued to function as the central organ of government from that time. Later, he established nine ministerial colleges to replace the chaos of the many conflicting and overlapping departments that had grown up in the Kremlin. He sent Russians to study colleges abroad, and appointed westerners to his own colleges, so that they might offer their expertise to the Russian members. But if he expected that they would keep each other mutually in motion, like the wheels of a watch, he was mistaken. Russians quarreled with foreigners and with each other. Unless the Tsar was present, their arguments, indolence, and inattention frequently brought business to a standstill.

Peter's solution was to appoint a series of personal repre-

sentatives to activate the others. He made Pavel Yaguzhinsky, a hardworking and energetic official, the Procurator
General of the Senate and told its members, "Here is my
eye, through whom I will see everything; he knows my in-
tentions and wishes. What he considers to be for the
general good, you are to do." He did not realize that the
use of such "eyes" undermined the independence and
initiative he so envied in the Swedish administration. What
he created instead, in a very rudimentary and imperfect
form, was a system of official espionage suggestive of the
Communist Party under Stalin.

Peter borrowed from the west to create the form of
a European bureaucracy, but he looked to the Muscovite
past for the means of staffing it. "In our state of Muscovy,
the serving men of every grade serve," runs the preamble
of a seventeenth-century decree, "and no one owns land for
nothing." The words express the formula by which the
Tsars exacted service from the landlords in return for grant-
ing them privileges over their serfs.

Peter took the old formula and extended it further. His
nobles must not only serve, but educate themselves for
service. He sent them abroad to study at their own expense.
He ordered them into his new academies. He founded
"cipher schools" to teach the three R's and decreed that
the sons of all landowners should attend them from the
ages of ten to fifteen.

In 1722 the establishment of the Table of Ranks brought
to its logical conclusion a process that had been evolving
for three centuries. It imposed obligatory lifelong state
service on all ranks of the nobility. It established fourteen
equivalent grades in the military, naval, and civil service
and required that even princes of the most exalted families

should begin at the lowest grade and work their way up the ladder. The Table of Ranks offered the privileges of nobility to anyone who performed state service and made service to the state the principal basis for privilege.

Peter also completed the subordination of the church to the state. After the death of the Patriarch Adrian, he avoided appointing a new Patriarch, and in 1721, he abolished the Patriarchate altogether. In its place, he created the Holy Synod as a sort of college of religious affairs. Its members were all appointed by the Tsar and presided over by a Procurator who was "the Tsar's eye."

In the end, it was the peasantry who carried the heaviest burden of the new state. In the first year of the Northern War, government expenditures were double what they had been when Peter came to the throne. By 1724, they had tripled. Peter had no way of borrowing money. In such a primitive economy, it had to be strictly pay-as-you-go, and it was the peasants who paid.

All the new taxes devised by the "profit makers" were inadequate to meet expenses, until Peter decided to adapt a version of the head tax he had seen in France. The "soul tax," as it was called, was to be levied on every male "soul" in the country. Nobles, churchmen, and certain privileged merchants were exempt. All others must pay. A census was conducted by the army with such merciless thoroughness that it took five years to complete. Evasion was punishable by death, and the use of torture often made the process seem more like an inquisition than a census. Finally, in 1724, the soul tax was collected for the first time. It was paid by 5,400,000 peasants and 169,000 townsmen. The tax was not scaled or graduated to the individual's ability to pay. All were assessed the same arbitrary amount.

The soul tax provided half of the total government revenue and solved Peter's financial problem, but only at the cost of intensifying serfdom. Peasants were forbidden to leave their villages without passports signed by their masters. Landlords were made the collecting agents for the government, and since they made the village elders responsible for the soul tax, the elders assumed greater authority than ever over the life of the village. Their conservatism resisted innovations that would have made farming more productive. Periodically, they redistributed farm lands among the villagers, undermining their sense of private property and discouraging peasant initiative. Through the soul tax, Peter, the avowed enemy of custom, helped to tighten its grip on the great mass of his people.

Prince Vasily Golitsyn had dreamed of freeing the serfs, and Pososhkov advised the Tsar to introduce greater freedom as an incentive to greater productivity. Many foreigners observed that serfdom was a major obstacle to progress, and Peter was at least partially aware of its drawbacks. But he was in a hurry. He did not have time to free the serfs and wait for the benefits that freedom would bring. He wanted to modernize Russia in a single generation, and the only way he could pay for it was with more serfdom, not less.

Peter was what the historian Arnold Toynbee has called "the archetype of the autocratic westernizing reformer." He has furnished a pattern for the leaders of all the developing nations since his day, and none followed him more closely than Stalin, who "set out from 1928 to 1941 to do for Russia all over again what Tsar Peter had done for her about 230 years earlier." Stalin himself described Peter's program of modernization as "a unique attempt to leap out of the framework of backwardness." Yet Peter erected his modern state on the foundation or framework of the very backwardness he was seeking to leap out of. The modernizer was trapped in the traditions of Muscovy. Because he built on them, the weight of his modern military bureaucracy pressed the great mass of the Russian people even deeper into the backwardness of a primitive past.

Chapter 31

FATHER OF THE FATHERLAND

After the news of the Treaty of Nystadt, a delegation from the Senate begged Peter to take the titles of Emperor, the Great, and Father of the Fatherland. There is irony in the last. The Russian idea of a father was of a benevolent patriarch with a fine full beard and an aura of dignity and reverence for tradition. The restless and beardless Peter, striding about the dockyards or sweating over a forge, was a far cry from a Russian father figure.

Yet in his way Peter did act as a father to his people. He loved them and tried to reform them. Sometimes he reasoned and persuaded. More often he bullied and punished. Force was habitual with him. In later life, he carried a cudgel and did not hesitate to use it on even his ministers and magnates.

A prime target of his wrath was official dishonesty. Corruption was everywhere. A public office was commonly regarded as an opportunity for private gain. Of all Peter's assistants, only half a dozen were really honest. On one occasion, the outraged Tsar was in the act of drawing up a decree that would punish with hanging any official who had stolen enough to pay for the rope. Yaguzhinsky intervened. Did Peter wish to be an Emperor without subjects? "Do we not all steal, some more, some less, some privately, some without disguise?" Peter laughed and tore up the decree.

His greatest favorite was the worst offender. Peter had raised Menshikov to the rank of prince and bestowed huge estates on him, but the Prince's appetite only grew with what it fed on. It was impossible to do business with him without a bribe. Peter warned him repeatedly, but, partly because of Catherine's intercession and partly through his own weakness for the man, the Tsar never punished him as he deserved. Once, when he threatened to reduce him to his former trade of pie seller, the irrepressible Prince borrowed a tray from a vendor on the street and ran back to Peter and Catherine, calling, "Pies! Hot pies!" until they were both helpless with laughter.

To ferret out corruption, the Tsar established a class of official spies, called "fiscals." They became "the best-hated men in the empire." Nesterov, their chief, inspired dread. Informers were richly rewarded. Guards officers of the Preobrazhensky secret police were assigned to investigate and try cases.

Many of those punished had formerly been Peter's trusted advisers. Shafirov, a Senator, and Gagarin, the Governor of Siberia, were hanged. Others were disgraced, knouted, mutilated, or exiled. Yet despite the violence of these punishments, Peter failed to stamp out corruption. He lamented that while he could turn dice on his lathe with his chisel, "I cannot turn mules with my cudgel." The most that could be said of his efforts was that they changed the ethical climate. Official wrongdoing continued, but after Peter it was at least recognized as wrongdoing.

If he could not force men to be honest, perhaps he could force them to be active. He posted trusted men, often Guards officers, to act as "Tsar's eyes" in the colleges, and issued exact instructions as to the time and conduct of the meetings. "There shall be talk only of the matter at hand. Moreover, if someone begins to speak, another shall not interrupt, but shall allow him to finish, and then the other shall speak, behaving as is proper to honorable men and not like housewives trading in the market."

There is something touching in his patient spelling out of details, and Peter could be gentle and forgiving when he chose. Once Nepluev, the superintendent of docks, got drunk on his name day and was late to work next morning. Discovering that the Tsar was there ahead of him, he was frightened, but confessed the truth in spite of it. Peter put his hand on the young man's shoulder and thanked him for his honesty. "God will forgive you," he said. "There is no one who has not sinned. And now let us visit a woman in childbed."

The Tsar who could lay his cudgel across the shoulders of a Senator could also pay a call on the wife of a carpenter. At one moment, he would patiently encourage initiative with a homely parable. A servant who sees his master drowning ought not to ask himself "whether it was written down in his contract that he should pull him out of the water." But then he would turn suddenly arbitrary in a way that paralyzed the initiative he had been trying to stimulate. "You will pay with your head, if you interpret orders again!"

The state was to act as a protecting parent to Russia's

infant commerce and industry. Toward a new factory, it was "like a mother over a child," but the child must not be spoiled by sparing the rod. "Our people are like children, who never want to begin the alphabet unless they are compelled by their teacher. . . . So in manufacturing affairs, we must not be satisfied with mere suggestion. We must ask and even coerce." When Peter saw how much easier it was for Livonians to reap with scythes than it was for Russians to reap with sickles, he took a fatherly interest in introducing the new method, but he was not afraid to use compulsion, for "though a thing be good and necessary, our people will not do it, unless forced to it."

In Alexander Pushkin's memorable phrase, the decrees of earlier Tsars were "written with the knout." Peter's decrees also threatened terrible punishments for failure to obey them, but Peter added the novel persuasion of logical argument. He gave the reasons why a law was good and necessary. In St. Petersburg, cows, pigs, and goats should be accompanied by a herdsman, "as such cattle wandering in the streets and other places deface roads and spoil trees." It was forbidden to ride a horse without a bridle, "for an unbridled horse cannot quickly be curbed." The reasoning is naïve, but Peter was dealing with a childlike people, and he reasoned with them as with children.

He wanted to create "a police state," but he intended something far broader than the modern meaning of the term. He defined the police as "the soul of civil society" and assigned it a wide variety of functions. It "promotes good husbandry . . . plans and maintains cities and streets, prevents high prices . . . guards against diseases, sees to the cleanliness of streets and homes . . . cares for the beggars, the poor, the sick, the maimed . . . protects widows, orphans, foreigners . . . brings up the young according to the Lord's commandments in chaste purity and honest study." To what we consider normal police functions, Peter added sanitation, public health, price control, road construction, urban planning, welfare, child care, and education—in short, everything left outside the military sphere.

To improve commerce, Peter issued regulations for the packaging of hemp, the weaving of cloth, the working of leather, and the construction of river barges. To prevent fires, he established specifications for the building of ovens, the dimensions of chimneys, and the roofing of houses. He decreed how his subjects should dress and wear their hair. He intervened in the most intimate areas of his people's lives. Old Mother Russia had allowed her children to develop their own customs. The "Father of the Fatherland" created a state with both the right and the duty to prescribe how its children should live, learn, work, worship, and behave under all circumstances.

Chapter 32

THE LAST YEARS

During his last years, the improvement of St. Petersburg remained Peter's abiding preoccupation, and the city
grew by leaps and bounds. In 1714, Weber, the Hanoverian Ambassador, had called it "a heap of villages linked
together like some plantation in the West Indies." A
decade later, he described it as "a wonder of the world,
considering its magnificent palaces . . . and the short time
that was employed in building it."

Catherine entered into her husband's ambitions for his
capital. Once, when he returned from a cruise in the Baltic,
she reported she had discovered a charming site for a summer palace about eight miles from the city. They set off to
inspect it next day, and to the Tsar's surprise, drove up to
a fine two-story stone palace set in a landscaped garden.
It was called Tsarskoe Selo and Catherine had had it built
completely without his knowledge. She led him to a window commanding a view of St. Petersburg on the horizon
and toasted his health as eleven cannon fired a salute in the

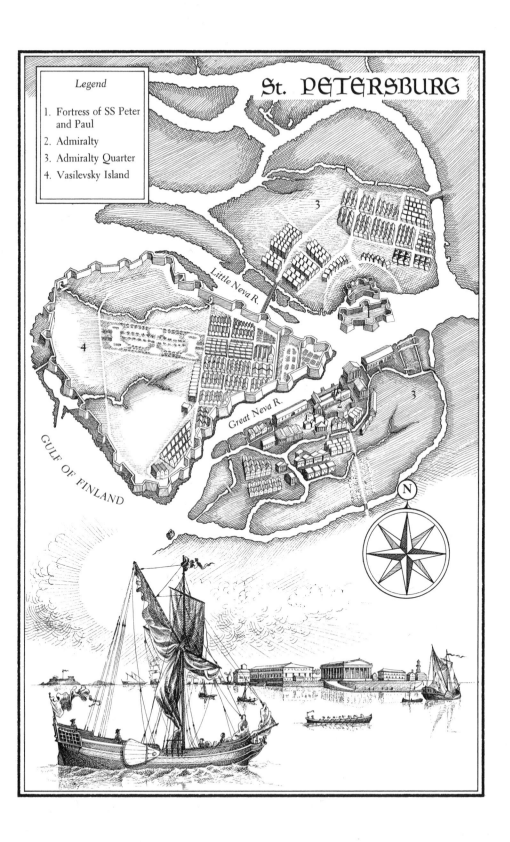

St. PETERSBURG

Legend

1. Fortress of SS Peter and Paul
2. Admiralty
3. Admiralty Quarter
4. Vasilevsky Island

Little Neva R.

Great Neva R.

GULF OF FINLAND

N

garden. Although he later preferred the palace of Peterhof, closer to the water, he pronounced this one of the happiest days of his life.

The expansion of St. Petersburg seldom seemed as effortless as the building of Tsarskoe Selo. Construction difficulties were enormous. All the materials had to be brought from the interior. The ground was so marshy that buildings of any size had to be raised on pilings, like the palaces of Venice.

Peter decided to make Vasilevsky Island the center of the city and ordered Trezzini to draw a master plan that would give it the appearance of Amsterdam. He commanded his ministers to build there. Later, he decreed that all nobles who owned forty or more serf households should construct residences on the island. Those with one hundred fifty or more peasant households had to build two-story structures in stone or brick. To aid them, the Tsar established sawmills and factories that made bricks and tiles. To expedite transport from the interior, he planned a canal to skirt Lake Ladoga, where violent storms frequently wrecked the barges. It was years in the building and was described as "the bottomless pit in which innumerable Russian subjects perish," but Peter persisted.

Long before the canal was finished in 1732, Peter had shifted most of the trade from Archangel to St. Petersburg by imperial decree. He forced the great merchants to live in the capital. He nearly doubled the duties for Archangel, and established quotas for key products that had to be exported from St. Petersburg. At different times, half, two thirds, or all of Russia's hemp, hides, caviar, tar, and potash had to be funneled through the new port. Only one ship traded there in 1713. There were 75 in 1720 and 180 in

1724. Meanwhile, from 1711 to 1725, the average annual shipping of Archangel declined from 154 to 50 ships.

The court, the foreign embassies, the government offices, the dockyards, and the trading companies each contributed to St. Petersburg's growing population. Russians grumbled at the expense and inconvenience. The cost of living was double that of Moscow. The winter was colder. The summer was hotter. The marshes breathed mist and malaria. Until the Neva froze, the only method of getting from island to island was by boat. But the Tsar insisted, and the city grew. By 1725, the population was nearly 100,000.

Peter worked to Europeanize the inhabitants. When he returned from Paris in 1717, he brought along plans, not only for buildings and gardens in the style of Versailles, but for social functions based on western models. He decreed that assemblies should be held two or three times a week in the city and personally drew up a list of 24 nobles to act as hosts. These assemblies were open to junior officers, merchants, and skilled artisans, along with the great magnates. They were to begin at four or five in the afternoon and continue until ten or eleven. Guests could come or go at will during these hours. The host need not greet each new arrival personally, but he was expected to provide for dancing, cards, and chess, with rooms set aside for parlor games, smoking, and conversation. Gambling was forbidden, and to avoid the drunkenness of most Russian entertainments, the host served only tea or water.

Yet the Tsar himself entertained in quite a different style. Weber, the Hanoverian envoy, described his treatment of a group of foreign ambassadors at the summer palace of Peterhof. Peter so pressed them with wine at dinner, "that on rising from the table, we could scarcely keep our legs, and when we had been obliged to drain quite a quart apiece from the hands of the Tsaritsa, we lost our senses entirely and, in that condition, they carried us out in different places, some to the garden, some to the woods, while the rest lay on the ground here and there. At four o'clock, they woke us up and again invited us to the summer house, where the Tsar gave us each an ax and beckoned us to follow him."

For three hours, Peter kept his foreign guests chopping in a young wood to clear a vista to the sea. When they had finished, "the fumes of the wine had been entirely evaporated," but after dinner, "the Tsar served a drink so strong that we were taken to our beds unconscious. . . . On the following day, none of us could remember who brought us home. . . . Breakfast consisted of a good glass of vodka, and afterward we were taken to the foot of a hill, made to mount some wretched country nags without saddles or stirrups, and ride about for an hour in the sight of Their Majesties, who stood at the window. . . . At dinner again, for the fourth time, we had to drink freely."

Peter may have been revenging himself on Weber and the other envoys for the diplomatic opposition of their courts to Russian interests in the Baltic, but his sense of humor was often cruel without cause. He forced an official who disliked his favorite Hungarian wine to drink so much of it that his servants had to drag him out into the snow to revive him. At the wedding banquet of Prince Golovin's daughter, the Tsar pushed one jelly after another into the mouth of the protesting Prince in the sight of the whole company. At his own banquets, he frequently posted guards to keep his guests at the table, while he went off to refresh himself with an hour's nap.

Catherine was the best leaven for Peter's fits of temper. She often interceded with pleas of mercy for those who had offended him. When he was suffering from one of the terrible headaches that threatened an outburst of violence, she would take his head into her lap and gently massage his temples until he fell into a doze. For hours, she would sit motionless so as not to disturb the sleeping Tsar, and when he awoke refreshed, the twitches and spasms that had been convulsing his movements were gone. At other times, she aroused in him something very like gallantry. When she sent him a pair of spectacles, he responded with a gift of jewelry and wrote, "Really on both sides, the presents are suitable. You send me wherewith to help my old age, and I send you wherewith to adorn your youth."

The Tsar continued to live simply. If he had to entertain, he used Catherine's or Menshikov's palace. He wore old clothes and had few attendants. He carried important papers in the pocket of his coat, which he rolled up and used as a pillow at night. He rose at three or four in the morning and worked with his secretaries or ministers. Later, he went off for an hour or two at the Admiralty dockyard. He dined at eleven, napped, and rose to dictate to his secretaries or inspect progress on some new construction. He was generally in bed by ten.

His hours are partly explained by the northern latitude. In summer, it was nearly always light. In winter, the sun rose at nine and set at three, but fog and storm could keep it dark all day. Peter's schedule ignored the difference between winter and summer, and, once it was established, ignored the differences in other climates and countries. He kept to the same hours in Paris and London.

In summer, he went sailing on the Neva and ordered his

nobles to join him. He banned the use of oars, so that everyone would learn to sail, but when the Polish Ambassador and one of his own physicians were drowned in consequence, he relaxed this prohibition.

He suffered increasingly from a painful condition of the kidneys and bladder, but refused to slacken his pace. At fifty, he set off down the Volga for a campaign against Persia, and took Catherine with him. He was afraid the Turks would take advantage of Persia's internal disorders to occupy the Caspian coast and wanted to forestall them. In July, 1722, he sailed into the Caspian with a fleet manned by 5,000 sailors and carrying 22,000 infantry. A large force of cavalry simultaneously advanced along the western shore. He took Derbent, Baku, and Resht, but prudently withdrew his main army to Astrakhan by the end of the year.

On his way home to St. Petersburg, he picked up the little sailboat in which he had first ventured on the Yauza thirty-five years before. In 1723, in the harbor at Kronstadt, with four admirals rowing and himself at the tiller, the "Grandsire of the Russian Fleet" passed in review before 22 ships of the line and 200 galleys firing thunderous broadsides in salute.

Frugal as he was himself, Peter insisted that Catherine keep a brilliant court. She was attended by a full complement of gentlemen of the bedchamber, ladies in waiting, pages, grooms, and an orchestra of musicians. While Peter went around in an old coat, her wardrobe held gowns by the thousands.

The court had a fondness for both dwarfs and giants. A dwarf enlivened the banquet celebrating the birth of Catherine's third son by bursting unexpectedly from a huge pastry to offer a toast to the Tsarevich Peter. Another time, seventy-two dwarfs staged a mock wedding in imitation of the marriage of Tsarevna Anna to the Duke of Courland and were afterward made roaring drunk. The French giant Nicholas was wed to a Finnish giantess at a gala masquerade. Negroes were objects of curiosity, and Catherine had several in attendance at her court. Peter took a particular fancy to a certain Ibrahim Hannibal, whom he sent to Paris to study. He later became a general and was an ancestor of Russia's first great poet, Alexander Pushkin.

One reason for the display of Catherine's court was Peter's anxiety for the succession. He had been deeply grieved by the death of the infant Tsarevich Paul, but he had taken comfort in the continued development of their little Petrushka. On hearing that he had cut his fourth tooth, he wrote Catherine, "God grant he cut all so well and that we may see him grow up, thus rewarding us for our former grief over his brothers." But in 1719, the year after the death of Alexis, little Peter followed his brothers to the grave. Catherine had two more sons, but both were stillborn.

In 1722, Peter issued a decree that the Tsar could name whomever he wished as his successor, but failed to name one. He seems never to have considered his daughters, Anna and Elizabeth, though they had grown into intelligent and well-educated girls. In the fall of 1723, he showed the drift of his mind by proclaiming that, in honor of her many services to the country, Catherine should be crowned Empress of Russia.

The coronation was performed with all the solemnity of ancient ritual. The court was moved to Moscow especially for the occasion. Only in the traditional home of the Tsars, in the third Rome, would the ceremony command the prestige Peter wished for it. Catherine's gown was ordered from France, and even the frugal Peter wore a coat embroidered in gold and silver. With his own hands, the Tsar set the crown on his wife's head, and to further enlist the allegiance of her people, he pardoned many petty criminals and exiles.

As he had ornamented his Empress, so he ornamented his capital. The history of Russia up to the revolution can be told in terms of three cities. The period before the Mongol Conquest centers on Kiev. The middle era belongs to Moscow. With the founding of St. Petersburg, Peter launched Russia into a new age, and he took great pains with its beautification.

The fountains Leblond designed for the palace of Peterhof are still a delight to visitors from all parts of the world. A German architect made Menshikov's palace the most splendid in the city. Peter decreed the construction of twelve great government buildings on the banks of Vasilevsky Island.

The use of western architects produced a style more appropriate to Holland or Italy than to Russia. Large glass windows were laid out in geometric patterns on rectangular facades. Their design lacked the exuberant fantasy of the tent roofs, onion domes, cupolas, and spires of Moscow. The old capital had grown for centuries in the cultural soil of Muscovy. St. Petersburg was born like Minerva from the head of a Russian Zeus. Conceived by western reason, it was built by Tsarist autocracy. The graceful stone buildings of a European capital gave no hint of the rough log pilings that supported them in the mud, or of the bodies of thousands of bearded serfs crushed beneath their weight.

In the summer of 1724, Peter's chronic ailment became acute. At fifty-two, he agreed to an operation to perforate his bladder through the wall of the lower abdomen. Using vodka as his only anesthetic, he kept himself from crying out; but his grip left deep bruises on the doctors who held his hands during the operation. For weeks he was in acute pain, but as soon as he began to feel better, he ignored the advice of his physicians.

He took a trip to Lake Ladoga to inspect work on the canal. At Olonetz he worked at the forge. In November, while sailing on the Gulf of Finland, he sighted a ship aground and in danger of capsizing in stormy seas. Taking charge of the rescue operations, he jumped into the water and spent several hours waist-deep in the freezing waves. Immediately afterward, he was stricken with fever and forced to return to St. Petersburg.

Still, he would not rest. He conducted an investigation of corruption and sentenced a court chamberlain to death. Simultaneously, he worked on plans for the Academy of Sciences and revised the rules and rituals of the All Drunken Synod. He remained a curious mixture of reformer, scientist, and buffoon right to the end.

On January 27, 1725, infection forced him to a sickbed. For days, he sank alarmingly. In a lucid moment, realizing that he might die without having named a successor, he asked his daughter Elizabeth for pen and paper. When he had scrawled a few words, the pen fell from his fingers. He had written only, "Give all to." The rest was blank. He never regained consciousness. In the early hours of the following morning, February 7, 1725, at the age of fifty-two, with his beloved Catherine by his side, he died.

Conclusion

THE FLAW OF GREATNESS

Peter's detractors argue that every one of his innovations had a precedent in the reign of an earlier Tsar. Ivan the Terrible had established a printing press. Boris Godunov had sent nobles to study abroad. The Slavonic Greek–Latin Academy had been founded under Peter's half brother, Fyodor. Even in the creation of the Russian navy, Peter's father had pioneered the way. Brandt, the Dutch carpenter who taught Peter to sail, had been hired by Tsar Alexis to build a ship for the navigation of the Caspian. On the basis of such evidence, some historians argue that Russia was already on the road to westernization and would have come to it even without Peter.

But she would not have come to it so suddenly. Evolution is not the same as revolution. It was the pace, scope, and violence of Peter's reforms that made them revolutionary. Moreover, the revolution was personal. He not only sent others abroad, but went himself. He not only hired foreign shipwrights, but built ships with his own hands.

Instead of merely importing a printing press, he learned to print and selected what was to be printed. He became the personal instrument and the embodiment of change.

He made giant strides in the field of education. He set up the Academy of Sciences. He founded schools of navigation, artillery, and engineering in the capital, and elementary or "cipher" schools in the provinces. He forced his nobles to study abroad. He established the first Russian newspaper. He redesigned the Russian alphabet to adapt it to movable type and saw to the translation and publication of western books. He impelled Russia from a manuscript culture toward a print culture, and after Peter, it could never again return to the intellectual climate of ancient Muscovy.

Except for his father's support of Nikon's reforms, earlier Tsars had interfered in the conduct of private life only on the side of custom. Peter admitted no such limits to his power. He prescribed new forms of behavior that defied hallowed traditions. Liberating upper-class women from the terem, he revolutionized marriage. He substituted a "German" for a Russian calendar. He told people where they must live and how they must construct their houses. He decreed their dress, their hair style, and even the use of their leisure hours. The image of the old Tsarism had been of a bearded and benevolent Byzantine patriarch, dignified and distant. The symbol of the new Russia was a clean-shaven and sharp-eyed "German" policeman, regulating and spying into everything. Under Peter, Russia's first regularly organized secret police stamped political life with a character that endures to this day.

The police state regulated commerce as well as custom.

During Peter's reign, foreign trade quadrupled, but this increase owed less to his mercantile policy than to his military conquest of ports like Riga, where a thriving commerce already existed. Peter managed to expand the trade of St. Petersburg only by ruining that of Archangel, and he never secured a significant share of that trade for native merchants. During his life and long afterward, western nations dominated trade with Russia as thoroughly as if she had been an overseas colony, exchanging raw materials for the finished goods she could not manufacture for herself.

The great exception to Russian dependence on the west was military. Peter saw clearly that unless he could modernize his arms production, Russia would remain a second-class nation. Earlier Tsars had opened iron mines, powder mills, and gun foundries, but Peter manufactured armament on a huge scale. In a single generation, his heavy industry outstripped that of far more advanced nations. His methods were despotic. The thousands of forced laborers drafted into his mines and factories were little better than industrial slaves, but iron production soared to more than three times that of England and helped to raise Russia to the rank of a great power.

To mobilize the resources of a primitive economy, Peter built on the achievements of his predecessors. The abolition of the Patriarchate and substitution of the Holy Synod institutionalized the state control of the church won by his father. The soul tax was an intensification of the serfdom that had been growing and spreading for centuries. The Table of Ranks was the final and logical step in a long evolution of state service. Yet the combination and culmination of these trends created a new kind of state that bound all classes to lifelong service and made all privileges dependent on such service.

Such a state required a powerful leader at its center. In the dynastic confusion that followed Peter's death, no fewer than seven monarchs ascended the throne in thirty-seven years. Four of them were women, whose rule was grudgingly accepted in a patriarchy. Of the three males, two were minors and the third was mentally unbalanced.

Peter's immediate successor was his wife, Catherine, the first Russian Empress. Two years later, her death brought to the throne Peter's grandson, the twelve-year-old son of Alexis, Peter II. In 1730, he was followed by Anna, the daughter of Peter's half brother Ivan V. In 1740, the infant great-grandson of this same Ivan—Anna's grand-nephew—was proclaimed Ivan VI. A year later, he was deposed by Peter's daughter, who became Empress Elizabeth. After her death in 1762, another Peter, the unstable son of Peter's daughter Anna, reigned briefly as Peter III, but was soon murdered with the probable connivance of his German wife, who succeeded him as Catherine II, later called Catherine the Great.

During these shifts and seizures, the Guards became, like the Streltsy of Peter's youth, the essential power base for the throne. To court their favor, successive monarchs granted special privileges to the nobles, whose class the Guards represented. In 1762, the nobles won total emancipation from the service forced on them by the Table of Ranks, but retained their rights over the serfs in full force.

Peter's program of westernization had deepened the division he found in the Russian people. The emancipation of the nobles from state service split the nation in two. The aristocracy, the army, and the bureaucracy became increasingly European. The peasantry, the clergy, and the merchant class lived in the old Muscovite way. The privileged ruling class shaved and dressed in the western style, built German or Italian villas landscaped with English gardens, and spoke French in preference to Russian. The bearded mass of the peasantry, groaning under a serfdom that became progressively harsher through the century, was a separate and oppressed people. Even before the Napoleonic invasion of 1812, they seemed to have been conquered and enslaved by a western army of occupation.

The intelligentsia reflected this division in the Russian people. The pro-western faction was ashamed of Russian backwardness and held that the only remedy was further westernization. They were opposed by the Slavophiles, who argued that westernization had alienated Holy Russia from her spiritual and cultural roots. Salvation lay not in the science and reason of the west, but in the purity and piety of Greek Orthodoxy. The star of the third Rome must rise in the east.

Westernizers glorified Peter, and Slavophiles condemned him; but his vision was broader than either group recognized. He had gone to school in the west to make war on the west, but his goals were not exclusively western. He fought on the Caspian Sea as well as the Baltic. He sent embassies and expeditions into Persia, central Asia, and China as well as to Europe. He ordered two frigates to Madagascar by way of the Cape of Good Hope and dreamed of a maritime commerce with India. He commissioned Vitus Bering on the Alaskan exploration that opened North America to Russian colonization. The global grandeur of his schemes was worthy of the Emperor of a third Rome.

He attempted far more than he could achieve in a lifetime. At his death, the Ladoga Canal was only half built. The new government buildings and the Academy of Sciences were barely begun. The dockyards at Voronezh and the abandoned Don-Volga canal were already crumbling in neglect. Peter had tried to do too much too fast. He was an impetus to the future, rather than its architect. He was forever making new beginnings in the hope that time would bring them to completion.

He expressed the essence of this hope in refuting critics of the Academy of Sciences who argued that such an academy was premature until there was an adequate school system to provide it with students. Peter countered with a homely parable, in which he likened himself to a farmer with a crop of wheat to grind: "But I have no mill, and there is not enough water close by to build a water mill. But there is water enough at a distance, only I shall have no time to make a canal, for the length of my life is uncertain, and, therefore, I am building the mill first and have only given orders for the canal to be begun, which will the better force my successors to bring water to the completed mill."

In this instance, his optimism proved justified. Within a few years, the Academy of Sciences was nurturing the genius of the great mathematician, philosopher, and historian, Mikhail Lomonosov. Yet, in many instances, Peter's attempt to "force my successors to bring water to the completed mill" imposed a terrible burden.

The very magnitude of his ambition may have been Peter's greatest defect. Undertaking the superhuman, he became less than humane. He was so dazzled by his hopes for the future that he was blind to their present cost. The imagined beauty of St. Petersburg was more real to him than the sufferings of tens of thousands who lost their lives in building it. His programs of construction caused nearly as much human misery as the devastation of his wars.

Peter was a living paradox, a builder and a destroyer, a visionary and a pragmatist, a genius and a buffoon. He was both flexible and adamant, frugal and prodigal, patient and passionate, magnanimous and merciless, self-sacrificing and self-centered. He went from one extreme to the other, a giant of a man, with appetites, endowments, and ambitions to match. "God has made the rivers to flow in one way," argued a conservative boyar who opposed the Don-Volga canal, "and it is presumption in man to think to turn them another." Peter's greatness was flawed by a thoroughly Promethean presumption. In the Greek myth, Zeus punished Prometheus, but allowed mankind to keep the fire he had stolen from Heaven. The Russian Prometheus went unpunished, while the vengeance of history fell on those he had meant to elevate. It was the Russian people who paid the price for the flaw in Peter's greatness.

HOUSE OF ROMANOV

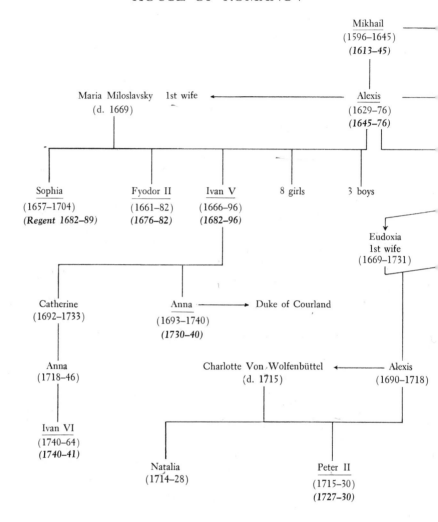

Mikhail
(1596–1645)
(1613–45)

Maria Miloslavsky   1st wife   ←   Alexis
(d. 1669)   (1629–76)
                                     (1645–76)

Sophia   Fyodor II   Ivan V   8 girls   3 boys
(1657–1704)   (1661–82)   (1666–96)
(Regent 1682–89)   *(1676–82)*   *(1682–96)*

Eudoxia
1st wife
(1669–1731)

Catherine   Anna   →   Duke of Courland
(1692–1733)   (1693–1740)
                       (1730–40)

Anna   Charlotte Von Wolfenbüttel   ←   Alexis
(1718–46)   (d. 1715)   (1690–1718)

Ivan VI
(1740–64)
(1740–41)

Natalia   Peter II
(1714–28)   (1715–30)
                       (1727–30)

Dates in italics indicate reign.

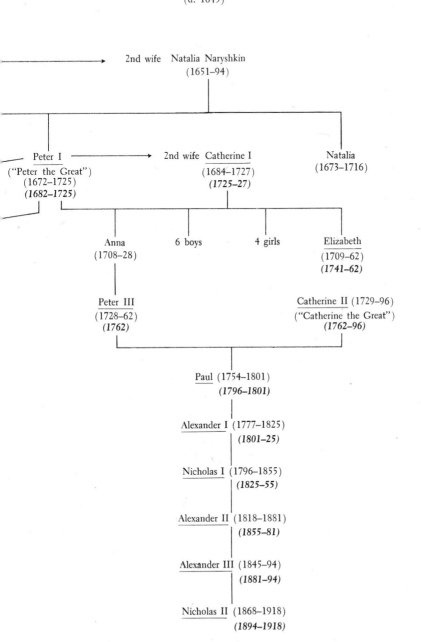

Eudoxia Streshnev
(d. 1645)

2nd wife   Natalia Naryshkin
(1651–94)

Peter I
("Peter the Great")
(1672–1725)
(1682–1725)

2nd wife   Catherine I
(1684–1727)
(1725–27)

Natalia
(1673–1716)

Anna
(1708–28)

6 boys

4 girls

Elizabeth
(1709–62)
(1741–62)

Peter III
(1728–62)
(1762)

Catherine II (1729–96)
("Catherine the Great")
(1762–96)

Paul (1754–1801)
(1796–1801)

Alexander I (1777–1825)
(1801–25)

Nicholas I (1796–1855)
(1825–55)

Alexander II (1818–1881)
(1855–81)

Alexander III (1845–94)
(1881–94)

Nicholas II (1868–1918)
(1894–1918)

THE ROMANOVS

ALEXIS (1629–76), the second of the Romanov Tsars, Peter's intelligent, conscientious, and devout father.

MARIA MILOSLAVSKY (d. 1669), the first wife of Tsar Alexis and mother of fourteen children, including Sophia, Fyodor, and Ivan.

SOPHIA (1657–1704), daughter of Maria, Peter's half sister and his elder by fifteen years. As fat and ugly as she was well-educated and shrewd, she acted as regent for Ivan and Peter from 1682 to 1689, when she was confined to a convent for life.

FYODOR (1661–82), son of Maria, Peter's older half brother. He succeeded Alexis as Fyodor II in 1676. Although he was intelligent and good-hearted, his youth, innocence, and poor health made him a tool of his family and favorites throughout his brief reign.

IVAN (1666–96), the youngest son of Maria, Peter's older half brother. Chronically ill and perhaps mentally retarded, he was nominally joint Tsar with Peter from 1682 until his death, but played no active role in affairs.

NATALIA NARYSHKIN (1651–94), second wife of Alexis and mother of Peter and his younger sister, "Natasha."

PETER (1672–1725), Tsar from 1682 until his death. After his victory over Sweden in 1721, he took the titles of Emperor, the Great, and Father of the Fatherland.

EUDOXIA LOPUKHIN (1669–1731), Peter's first wife. Timid, uneducated, conservative, and religious, she was badly matched to

Peter. Married to him in 1689, she bore him her only child, Alexis, in the following year.

ALEXIS (1690–1718), the only child of Eudoxia and the only one of Peter's seven sons to survive childhood. Indolent, superstitious and terrified of his formidable father, he gave the impression that he would undo Peter's life work if he should come to the throne.

CATHERINE SKAVRONSKY (1684–1727), Peter's second wife, a Livonian peasant who became the first Empress of Russia. Generous, courageous, and abounding with good health and good humor, she was an ideal wife for Peter. She bore him twelve children, but none of her six sons and only two girls, Anna and the future Empress Elizabeth, grew to maturity.

CHARLOTTE VON WOLFENBÜTTEL (d. 1715), a German princess, the sister-in-law of the Austrian Emperor, and the wife of Tsarevich Alexis. She survived the birth of a son, the future Tsar Peter II, by only a few days.

OTHER IMPORTANT PERSONS

ADRIAN, Patriarch of the Russian Church 1690–1700. Because Peter appointed no successor and later abolished the office, he was the last Russian Patriarch.

APRAXIN, FYODOR, Governor General of Archangel in 1693, later rose to rank of Admiral, captured Vyborg in Finland, 1710.

AUGUSTUS II (1670–1733), Elector of Saxony who, with Peter's support, was elected King of Poland in 1697. Bluff, handsome, and physically powerful, he was Peter's unreliable and occasionally disloyal ally in the Northern War against Sweden.

BRANDT, KARSTEN, a Dutch carpenter and shipwright, Peter's first teacher in the art of sailing and shipbuilding.

BULAVIN, a lesser chieftain of the Don Cossacks, who ambushed and massacred the troops of Prince Yury Dolgoruky to open the rebellion of 1707.

BUTURLIN, PRINCE IVAN, an older friend of Peter, whom he customarily named "King of Poland" in his war games.

CARMARTHEN, PEREGRINE OSBORNE, Marquis of Carmarthen, English admiral and ship designer, who entertained Peter in England.

CHARLES XII (1682–1718), King of Sweden, who came to the throne at fifteen. A willful, daring, and arrogant youth, he showed unexpected military prowess in the Northern War and was dubbed alternately "the Alexander of the North" and "the Madman of the North."

DOLGORUKY, a distinguished boyar family, many of whose members served the Russian state in Peter's day.

> **PRINCE IVAN,** died of wounds received in a sham fight, 1691.

> **PRINCE VASILY,** general, who crushed the Bulavin rebellion in 1708, subsequently exiled for his secret support of Tsarevich Alexis.

> **PRINCE YAKOV,** ambassador, who brought the sixteen-year-old Peter an astrolabe from western Europe in 1688.

> **PRINCE YURY,** general, ambushed and murdered by Bulavin in 1707.

EFROSINIA, Finnish serf girl, who became the mistress of Tsarevich Alexis and later betrayed him to Peter.

FREDERICK I, Elector of Brandenburg, whose energy, ambition, and guile established him as first King of Prussia in 1701.

GOLITSYN, a distinguished boyar family.

> **PRINCE BORIS,** conservative aristocrat, one of the leaders of Peter's party against Sophia in 1689.

> **PRINCE VASILY,** one of the most enlightened and liberal Russians of his day, who became the principal minister and lover of Sophia and shared her downfall in 1689.

GOLOVIN, a great boyar family.

> **ARTEMON,** a general at the siege of Azov (1695–96).

> **FYODOR,** one of the three official ambassadors on the Great Embassy in 1697–98.

GORDON, PATRICK, Scottish soldier of fortune in the Russian army (1661–99). He was already a general when he taught young Peter the art of fireworks and became his trusted adviser.

KHOVANSKY, prince and commander of the Streltsy, whose intrigues led Sophia to behead him in 1682.

LEFORT, FRANZ, Swiss adventurer and soldier of fortune, who became a Russian general. He was Peter's closest and most influential favorite until his death in 1699.

LEIBNIZ, GOTTFRIED WILHELM, the geat German mathematician and philosopher, who became an enthusiastic admirer of Peter and advised him on legal and educational reforms.

MATVEYEV, ARTEMON, the able and liberal minister of Tsar Alexis, who introduced him to his ward and kinswoman, Natalia Naryshkin, Peter's mother. He was murdered in the Streltsy riots.

MAZEPA, Ataman of the Cossacks of the Ukraine, who betrayed Peter and joined Charles XII in 1708.

MENSHIKOV, ALEXANDER, a former pie vendor who rose to the rank of Prince and Governor General of St. Petersburg. Courageous, clever, and thoroughly corrupt, he replaced Lefort as Peter's great favorite after Lefort's death, and introduced the Tsar to his future wife, Catherine.

MILOSLAVSKY, IVAN, older brother of Maria, the first wife of Tsar Alexis. The cunning, insolent, and unscrupulous leader of the Miloslavsky clan against the Naryshkin branch of the royal family.

MONS, ANNA, the blonde, blue-eyed, and buxom daughter of a German goldsmith who became Peter's mistress in the German Suburb about 1690.

NARYSHKIN, the family of Natalia, Peter's mother.

> **IVAN,** Natalia's older brother, who was tortured and hacked to pieces by the Streltsy.

> **LEV,** Peter's uncle, who helped to direct the strategy that overthrew Sophia and established Peter in his own right.

PATKUL, JOHANN, fiery Livonian noble and patriot, who sought his country's liberation from Sweden. Taking service first with Augustus in Saxony and later with Peter in Poland, he sought to spur their attack on Charles XII.

POSOSHKOV, IVAN, a former peasant, who earned a modest fortune through his activity in a variety of trades and wrote many illuminating descriptions and analyses of Russian life under Peter.

REPNIN, PRINCE NIKITA, an able military commander in the war with Sweden.

ROMODANOVSKY, PRINCE FYODOR, an older member of Peter's inner circle, who frequently played the role of "Mock Tsar" or "Prince Caesar" in ceremonies devised by Peter. He became head of Russia's first regularly-organized secret police.

SHAKLOVITY, FYODOR, commander of the Streltsy, whom Peter tortured and beheaded for his attempts to have Sophia crowned.

SHEIN, ALEXIS, a respected boyar whom Peter named Generalissimo of the army at Azov in 1696.

SHEREMETEV, BORIS, an experienced general under Peter's father, appointed commander-in-chief in Livonia in 1701.

TIMMERMANN, FRANZ, a Dutch merchant who taught Peter the necessary mathematics to use an astrolabe in 1688.

TOLSTOY, COUNT PETER, an accomplished diplomat, ambassador to Turkey, and Peter's special envoy to persuade the Tsarevich Alexis to leave his sanctuary in Naples.

TSYKLER, IVAN, colonel of the Streltsy, who turned against Sophia to win favor with Peter in 1689, but was convicted and executed for treason in 1697.

VINIUS, ANDREW, whose Dutch father had founded the Tula Arms Works, and who was appointed Postmaster General by Tsar Alexis. Under Peter, he opened iron mines and worked wonders replacing the artillery lost at Narva until the Tsar discovered his profiteering and stripped him of his honors.

WEIDE, ADAM, a German who rose to the rank of general as one of Peter's most trusted officers.

WILLIAM III (1650–1702), simultaneously King of England and Staatholder of Holland, principal architect of several alliances designed to check the growing power of Louis XIV. His preoccupation with France made him unwilling to offer Peter an alliance against Turkey, but he proved a good host to the Tsar in England.

WITSEN, NICHOLAS, a Dutch merchant who had traveled widely in Russia and subsequently became Mayor of Amsterdam. He acted as a purchasing agent for Peter and arranged for him to work as a ship's carpenter on the East India wharf.

YAGUZHINSKY, PAVEL, one of the half-dozen officials in Peter's government who was known to be completely honest. Peter appointed him Procurator-General over the Senate.

YOACHIM, Patriarch of the Russian Church 1667–90, an arch-conservative who bitterly opposed westerners and western ideas.

ZOTOV, NIKITA, Peter's childhood tutor and later "Prince Pope" of the Tsar's "All Drunken Synod."

IMPORTANT DATES
IN EARLY RUSSIAN HISTORY

862 The legendary Rurik, a Viking prince, becomes ruler over the Slavs on the banks of the Dnieper.

988 Vladimir, Grand Prince of Kiev, is converted to Greek Orthodox Christianity, symbolizing Russia's incorporation into Europe on its eastern frontier.

1240 The Golden Horde of the Mongol Empire conquers Kiev and isolates Russia from contact with Europe.

1326 The Metropolitan of the Russian Church moves to Moscow, making it the religious capital of the country.

1453 Constantinople, "the second Rome," falls to the Turks, threatening the extinction of Greek Orthodox Christianity.

1480 Ivan the Great throws off the Mongol yoke, takes title of Tsar (Russian form of "Caesar") as heir to Byzantine Empire. Moscow becomes center of Greek Orthodoxy, "the third Rome."

1553 An English ship discovers Archangel, and Russia opens direct trade with the west.

1565–72 Ivan the Terrible's reign of terror crushes independent nobles and forces state service on all lords.

1598 The death of Tsar Fyodor I without male heirs leads to disputed succession, civil war, peasant revolts, and foreign invasion, the so-called Time of Troubles.

1610   The Poles capture Moscow.

1613   Having united to expel the foreigners, the representatives of the nobles and people choose Mikhail as the first of the ·Romanov Tsars.

1667   Patriarch Nikon is deposed by a church council, but his reforms are confirmed. The excommunication of the Old Believers shatters Russian religious unity forever.

1670–71   The revolt of Stenka Razin spreads a thousand miles up the Volga before it is crushed.

IMPORTANT DATES
IN THE LIFE OF PETER

1672   Birth of Peter, June 9.

1676   Death of Tsar Alexis. Succession of Peter's older half brother, Fyodor II.

1682   Death of Fyodor II. Streltsy riots. Coronation of Peter and older brother, Ivan, as joint Tsars under the Regency of Sophia.

1689   Marriage of Peter to Eudoxia Lopukhin. Peter's supporters overthrow Sophia.

1690   Birth of Tsarevich Alexis.

1693   Peter's first visit to Archangel.

1694   Death of Peter's mother, Natalia.

1695   Unsuccessful campaign against Azov.

1696   Death of half brother Ivan V. Peter sole Tsar. Capture of Azov.

1697   Departure of the Great Embassy.

1698   Peter in England. Alliance with Augustus II against Charles XII of Sweden. Divorce from Eudoxia. First attacks on beards, native dress, and segregation of women.

1698-99   Suppression of the Streltsy.

1700   Reform of Russian calendar. Declaration of war with Sweden, and defeat at Narva.

1701   Founding of the School of Mathematics and Navigational Sciences, first secular school in Russian history.

1703   Conquest of the Neva River and founding of St. Petersburg.

1704   Conquest of Dorpat and Narva.

1707   Outbreak of rebellion of Bulavin. Treaty of peace between Augustus II and Charles XII. Marriage of Peter and Catherine.

1708   Swedish invasion of Russia. Death of Bulavin. Defection of Mazepa, Cossack chief of Ukraine.

1709   Victory at Poltava.

1710   Conquest of Riga.

1711   Creation of Senate. Invasion of Turkey; defeat on the Pruth; loss of Azov. Marriage of Tsarevich Alexis to German princess.

1714   Naval victory over Swedes at Hangö.

1716   Disappearance of Alexis.

1717   Peter in Paris.

1718   Return, conviction, and death of Alexis. First Russian census. Ministerial "colleges."

1721   Abolition of the Patriarchate. Treaty of Nystadt with Sweden. Peter, "Emperor, the Great, Father of the Fatherland."

1722   Table of Ranks.

1722–23   War with Persia and conquest of eastern and southern shores of Caspian Sea.

1724   First collection of poll or "soul" tax. Coronation of Catherine as Empress.

1725   Establishment of Academy of Sciences. February 7, death of Peter at fifty-two.

BIBLIOGRAPHY

The books listed below are divided into three categories: those that focus directly on Peter the Great, accounts of Petrine Russia by British contemporaries, and background histories of various sorts. All are available in English.

1. Books on Peter the Great:

Grey, Ian, *Peter the Great*. Philadelphia, 1960.
   A good recent biography.
Klyuchevsky, Vasily, *Peter the Great*. New York, 1969.
   Based on lectures which Klyuchevsky gave at the University of Moscow around the turn of the century; a vivid portrait illuminated by many penetrating insights.
Raeff, Marc, ed., *Peter the Great: Reformer or Revolutionary*. New York, 1966.
   A collection of comments on Peter's successes or failures in various fields by a variety of authors, contemporaries as well as historians, Russians as well as westerners, Soviet Marxists as well as political moderates.
Schuyler, Eugene, *Peter the Great, Emperor of Russia*. New York, 1884.
   Still the most complete biography of Peter in English.

Sumner, B.H., *Peter the Great and the Emergence of Russia*. New York, 1951.

——, *Peter the Great and the Ottoman Empire*. Oxford, 1949.

Two books that give an admirable picture of Peter's program for the new Russia, his successes and his failures.

Tolstoy, Alexis, *Peter the Great*. London, 1936.

A biographical novel that vividly recreates the atmosphere, sights, sounds, and smells of Peter's Russia, and his life up to the victory at Narva in 1704.

2. There are a number of accounts of Russian life in Peter's day by westerners who traveled or lived in the country for one reason or another. Among those in English are the following:

Bell, John, *Travels from St. Petersburg in Russia to Various Parts of Asia*. Edinburgh, 1806.

An interesting account of travels in remote regions not generally associated with Peter's foreign policy.

Bridge, C.A.P., *History of the Russian Fleet during the Reign of Peter the Great*. London, 1899.

A detailed but not eminently readable account of naval events under Peter.

Bruce, Peter Henry, *Memoirs*. New York, 1782.

Memoirs of a Scottish soldier of fortune which give a flavor of military life in the Northern War.

Gordon, Patrick, *Passages from the Diary of General Patrick Gordon of Auchleuchries*. Aberdeen, 1859.

A diary of Peter's trusted military adviser covering thirty-eight years in the Russian service; suffers from editorial paraphrasing.

Perry, John, *The State of Russian under the Present Czar.*
London, 1716.
  By far the most colorful and informative account of
  Peter and Russia by an English observer.
Whitworth, Charles, *An Account of Russia as it was in
1710.* Strawberry Hill, 1758.
  A brief but illuminating picture of Russia as it seemed
  to the British ambassador.

3.   Below are listed a wide variety of books, all or parts of
which help to place Peter in the context of a broader
history.

Albion, Robert G., *Forests and Sea Power: The Timber
Problem of the Royal Navy, 1652–1862.* Cambridge, Mass.,
1926.
  A brilliant pioneering work exploring the importance of
  naval stores, and especially the masts of the Baltic, in
  the rivalry of the great maritime powers of Europe.
Billington, James, *The Icon and the Axe.* New York,
1968.
  An excellent cultural history of which early chapters give
  a vivid picture of the climate of Muscovy into which
  Peter was born.
Blum, Jerome, *Lord and Peasant in Russia.* Princeton, N.J.,
1961.
  An exhaustive study of the changing relations between
  nobles and peasants in Russia over a period of one thou-
  sand years.
Dorn, Frederick L., *Competition for Empire (1740–1763).*
New York, 1940.
  Although it deals with a later period, valuable for its

description of the competitive states' system of Europe into which Peter introduced Russia.

Earle, Edward Mead, ed., *Makers of Modern Strategy.* Princeton, N.J., 1943.

A brilliant military history of which the first chapters describe technical advances in the warfare of the west that posed a great challenge to Peter.

Hoetzsch, Otto, *The Evolution of Russia.* New York, 1966.

A good brief history of Russia, with excellent illustrations.

Horizon Editors, *History of Russia.* New York, 1970.

One-volume history of Russia, with a text by Ian Grey, copiously and excellently illustrated with more than four hundred fine reproductions and photographs.

Lyashchenko, P.I., *History of the National Economy of Russia to 1917.* New York, 1949.

An economic survey of Russian history by an outstanding Soviet authority.

Mavor, James, *An Economic History of Russia.* New York, 1914.

An economic history of pre-Soviet Russia, written before the overthrow of the Romanovs.

Putnam, Peter, ed., *Seven Britons in Imperial Russia, 1698–1812.* Princeton, N.J., 1952.

An anthology of the writings of British travelers during and after Peter's time, with explanatory remarks by the editor.

Raeff, Marc, *Origins of the Russian Intelligentsia.* New York, 1966.

A splendid social history of the development of a class that appeared in Russia as a result of Peter's reforms.

Reading, Douglas K., *The Anglo–Russian Commercial Treaty of 1734.* New Haven, Conn., 1938.

A book whose early chapters illuminate the character of Russian commerce as it developed under Peter.

Robinson, G.T., *Rural Russia under the Old Regime*. New York, 1949.
A solid history of the growth of the servile system under the Tsars.

Simmons, E.J., *English Literature and Culture in Russia, 1553–1840*. Cambridge, Mass., 1935.
A fascinating account of English influences in the westernization of Russia.

Steuart, Archibald F., *Scottish Influences in Russian History*. Glasgow, 1913.
Largely anecdotal material on the many Scottish soldiers, adventurers, engineers, and physicians who found their way into the service of Russia.

Sumner, B.H., *A Short History of Russia*. New York, 1949.
A comprehensive survey in the shortest possible space.

Toynbee, Arnold, *The World and the West*. New York, 1953.
A brilliant essay on the reaction of non-western peoples to aggression by the west that portrays Peter as the first autocratic reformer of a backward country.

Utechin, Serge V., *Russian Political Thought*. New York, 1964.
An excellent survey of Russian political thought from its beginning to the present.

Wolf, John B., *Emergence of the Great Powers: 1685–1715*. New York, 1951.
A treatment of the War of the Spanish Succession and the Northern War as related parts of the first true world war, embroiling all Europe in a conflict waged around the world.

INDEX

Format by Anne E. Brown
Set in 12 pt. Electra with cursive
Composed by Haddon Craftsmen, Inc.
Printed by The Murray Printing Company.
Bound by Haddon Craftsmen, Inc.
HARPER & ROW, PUBLISHERS, INCORPORATED